The Resilient Leader

Carey H. Peerman, PhD

The Resilient Leader:

A Foundational Guide to Building Resilient Leadership
Volume 1

Library of Congress Cataloging-in-Publication Data Control Number:
Name: Dr. Carey Peerman
Title: The Resilient Leader: A Foundational Guide to Building Resilient Leadership
The Resilient Leader: A Foundational Guide to Building Resilient Leadership
Description: Virginia, Dr. Carey Peerman, 2024 |Includes bibliographical reference.
Identifiers: ISBN: 978-1-7373745-3-4
Subjects: Business, Business Life - General & Miscellaneous, Business Life & Careers, Business Life & Skills, Personal Growth
Book cover design by Scott Newton, APEX Media Solutions, Inc.

Contents

Action/Reaction-How does action and reaction impact the
    development of resilience?
Knowledge-How does knowledge impact the development of
    resilience?
Strength-How does mental strength impact the development of
    resilience?

PART II – The Application of Resilient Leadership

THE WHO:
Who would want to become a resilient leader?
THE WHAT:
What is Resilience?
What factors impact Resilience Development?
What are the key tools of a resilient leader?
What is the survival guide to developing resilience?
What is mental fragmentation?
What relates mental fragmentation to resilience?
THE WHEN:
When are resilient leaders needed in teams or organizations?
When does a leader become a resilient leader?
THE WHERE:
Where are resilient leaders most needed?
Where are resilient leaders NOT needed?
THE WHY:
Why is resilience important to those in leadership roles?
THE HOW:
How is grit part of resilience development?
Are grit and mental toughness the same thing?
Is mental toughness the same as resilience?

How does resilience apply to psychological trauma?
How does resilience impact states of uncertainty?
How is hope part of resilience?
How does resilience help one overcome hardship?
How does resilience help establish a new normal?
How does resilience negate fear?
How are resilience and nourishing the soul related?

How does the act of suffering help to develop resilience?

How can the reserves of resilience sustain an individual?

How does trauma build on more trauma?

How is resilience related to well-being?

How does structure and routine help build resilience?

How does building resilience equal unparalleled times of self-growth?

How do spiritual convictions ground resilience?

How is loneliness curbed with resilience?

How are nature and resilience comparable?

How is resilience developed at an individual level?

How is resilience developed in leaders to nurture teams and foster strength?

How is resilience developed at an organizational level?

How does engagement create resilience at the organizational level?

How is resilience developed at the Community Level?

Acknowledgements

The time and energy devoted to the development of a book rests entirely on the support of those in your life circle. This book has been collaborative in nature because of the people who have given me the encouragement, guidance, and assistance I needed to take it from idea to publication.

It is with heartfelt gratitude that I extend my deepest appreciation to my pillars of strength: my husband, Robert, and son, Thomas, for their unwavering love and support. To my parents, Glenn and Connie, and sister, Erin, your encouragement and belief in me has been invaluable. Your steadfast support and inspirational presence have been a guiding force in my life's journey as a wife, mother, and educator. To Ellen Rachel, a cherished lifelong friend, you have been a constant source of joy and support. Thank you.

I also wish to acknowledge the exceptional leaders who have generously shared their wisdom with me, guiding and supporting me on my journey as a nurse, administrator, professor, consultant and author. Special thanks to my close group of friends, it takes a village, I love you all.

Lois for always believing I could achieve my dreams.
Leslie for being a friend on this journey that always gives sound advice.
Cathy for your special support, guidance, mentorship, and friendship.
Nancy for your friendship, chats, and always believing in me.
Lastly and especially Mary who is one of the smartest, most dedicated and prime examples of a resilient leader I have ever encountered - thank you.

Your embodiment of resilient leadership in your careers and lives is truly inspiring. You are the best, and I am profoundly thankful for your mentorship and influence.

In memory of my dear friend Anita, we were instantly connected and had great talks and times together. You were always there for me. I miss you, my friend. Until we meet again.

How To Use This Book

As a lifelong learner and now educator, I have always liked the idea of being given insights on how to utilize and/or apply the information I will learn. Whether it is a book, educational workshop, or even a conference, understanding how to maximize the learning experience ensures a more beneficial outcome.

With the above thought in mind, as you embark on the exploration of my first book in The Resilient Leader series, I encourage you to consider The Resilient Leader: A Foundational Guide to Building Resilient Leadership as your personal guide to be used to fortify your mental and emotional well-being. Actively engage with the principles presented and reflect on how you can apply them to your trajectory of becoming a resilient leader.

A helpful exercise during your study is to journal your personal insights and prospective goals from each chapter. Consider how you will apply the diverse questions and explanations into transformative action. Document these thoughts. Remember that the purpose of this book is to not just teach you concepts in resilience to empower your growth, but to encourage their application to your personal and professional life.

Also, a key strategy in learning concepts and making them a part of your inner being is to share what you have learned with others. This also opens the opportunity to compare the experiences of your peers to the foundational principles of resilient leadership. Ask yourself what lessons you can learn from their failures and successes.

At last, remember that the true power of this book lies not only in reading but in actively applying these principles to cultivate resilient leadership in your own unique way. I sincerely hope this guide can serve as a catalyst for positive change and a source of strength on your path to greater resilience and leadership of others.

PART I
The Basics of Resilient Leadership

Chapter 1
Introduction to Resilient Leadership

The History of Resilient Leadership

The concept of resilient leadership has its roots in the study of resilience, which emerged as a field of research in the 1970s. Researchers were interested in understanding how some people were able to overcome adversity and thrive despite difficult circumstances. This led to the development of the concept of resilience, which was originally applied in the context of individual psychology.

Over time, the concept of resilience began to be applied in other fields, including leadership. Researchers began to study leaders who were able to navigate complex and uncertain environments and identified a set of characteristics that these leaders shared. These characteristics included a willingness to take calculated risks, an ability to adapt to changing circumstances, and a focus on building strong relationships and networks.

In the early 2000s, the concept of resilient leadership began to gain traction in both academic and professional circles. This was in part due to a number of high-profile crises and disasters, such as the 9/11 terrorist attacks, the global financial crisis, and the Fukushima nuclear disaster, which highlighted the importance of resilience in leadership.

Today, resilient leadership is widely recognized as a critical skill for leaders in all sectors and industries. Resilient leaders are able to anticipate and respond to unexpected challenges and opportunities, while also building strong and sustainable organizations that can withstand and recover from crises. They are able to balance short-term needs with long-term goals and are committed to promoting the well-being and success of their organizations, their employees, and their communities.

Overall, the history of resilient leadership reflects a growing recognition of the importance of resilience in leadership, and an increasing understanding of the characteristics and behaviors that define resilient leaders. As organizations continue to face complex and uncertain environments, resilient leadership will likely become even more important in the years ahead.

Why Resilience Matters to Leaders

Resilience matters to leaders because it enables them to better navigate challenges and setbacks, and to lead their teams through difficult times. Leaders who possess resilience are better equipped to maintain a positive outlook and stay focused on their goals, even in the face of adversity. They are also better able to manage stress and bounce back from setbacks, which can help them to remain effective and productive over the long term.

Additionally, leaders who model resilience can inspire their team members to develop this skill, creating a more resilient organization as a whole. By demonstrating resilience, leaders can help their team members to feel more confident and empowered, even in difficult circumstances. This can lead to a more engaged and motivated team, which can in turn improve overall organizational performance.

Finally, resilience is particularly important in times of crisis or uncertainty, as it enables leaders to remain calm and focused in the face of chaos. By modeling resilience during these times, leaders can help their team members to feel more confident and secure, and to maintain a sense of stability in the organization. Overall, resilience is an essential skill for effective leadership, and leaders who prioritize this skill can create a more successful and sustainable organization.

Chapter 2
What Does Resilience Look Like?

Resilient Leadership Development Levels

Resilient Leadership consists of five development levels. Individual Resilience (IR) is the foundation from where Resilient Leadership Development begins. It is important to distinguish between the different levels, including their characteristics and application of each.

Individual Resilience: What does resilience look like at the individual level?

Resilience at the individual level can look different for each person, but there are some common characteristics that are often associated with resilience. Resilient individuals tend to maintain a positive outlook, even in the face of challenges or setbacks. They focus on their strengths and abilities, rather than their weaknesses and limitations. Resilient individuals are able to adapt to changing circumstances and adjust their strategies as needed. They are willing to try new approaches and take calculated risks.

Resilient individuals prioritize their own well-being and take steps to manage stress and maintain their physical and emotional health. They may engage in activities such as exercise, meditation, or hobbies that bring them joy and fulfillment. Resilient individuals have a strong support network, including friends, family, or colleagues who they can turn to for help and encouragement. They also may seek out professional support, such as therapy or coaching, when needed.

Resilient individuals are effective problem-solvers, able to identify and address challenges in a proactive and strategic way. They may seek out advice or input from others, but ultimately take responsibility for finding solutions to their problems. Furthermore, resilience at the individual level involves a combination of skills and characteristics that enable individuals to navigate challenges and setbacks with greater ease and effectiveness. By developing these skills, individuals can improve their overall well-being and success in all areas of life.

Resilient Leaders: What does resilience look like at the leader level?

Resilience at the leader level involves a set of skills and behaviors that enable leaders to navigate challenges, inspire their team members, and maintain a positive outlook even in difficult circumstances. Resilient leaders are emotionally intelligent, able to recognize and manage their own emotions and those of their team members. They are skilled at building strong relationships and creating a positive work culture.

Resilient leaders are able to adapt to changing circumstances and remain flexible in the face of uncertainty. They are willing to take calculated risks and try new approaches. Resilient leaders have a clear vision for their organization and set goals that are challenging but achievable. They are able to motivate and inspire their team members to work towards these goals. Resilient leaders are effective problem-solvers, able to identify and address challenges in a proactive and strategic way. They are able to see the big picture and develop creative solutions to complex problems.

Resilient leaders prioritize their own well-being and take steps to manage stress and maintain their physical and emotional health. They may engage in activities such as exercise, mindfulness, or hobbies that bring them joy and fulfillment. Lastly, resilient leaders are able to maintain a positive outlook, inspire their team members, and lead their organizations through difficult times. By developing these skills and characteristics, leaders can create a more resilient and successful organization.

Team Resilience: What does resilience look like at the team development level?

Resilience at the team development level involves creating a work environment where team members can work together effectively, adapt to change, and overcome challenges. Resilient teams have open and honest communication among team members. This includes the ability to provide constructive feedback and address conflicts in a productive manner. Resilient teams trust each other and collaborate effectively. They understand each other's strengths and weaknesses and work together to achieve common goals.

Resilient teams are able to adapt to changing circumstances and are willing to try new approaches when necessary. They are also able to manage stress and maintain a positive outlook in the face of uncertainty. Resilient teams are committed to learning and development. They are open to feedback and actively seek out opportunities for growth and improvement. Resilient teams provide support and empathy to each other. They understand that everyone may face challenges at some point, and work together to help each other through difficult times. Moreover, resilient teams are able to work together effectively and adapt to changing circumstances, which enables them to achieve better results and overcome challenges. By creating a work environment that supports resilience, leaders can help their teams to thrive and succeed in the long term.

Organizational Resilience: What does resilience look like at the organizational development level?

Resilience at the organizational development level involves creating a work environment that is able to adapt to change, navigate challenges, and achieve long-term success. Resilient organizations have strong, visionary leaders who are able to inspire their teams and lead through uncertainty.

Resilient organizations have a culture of open communication, where employees feel comfortable sharing their ideas and concerns. Resilient organizations foster a collaborative culture, where employees are encouraged to work together across departments and functions. Resilient organizations are committed to continuous learning and improvement, with opportunities for employee development and training. Resilient organizations are able to adapt to changing circumstances and are willing to embrace innovation and new approaches. Resilient organizations have effective risk management practices in place, with contingency plans and strategies for managing potential crises.

Resilient organizations prioritize employee well-being, with programs and policies in place to support physical and mental health. Resilient organizations have strong relationships with stakeholders, including customers, suppliers, and community partners. Overall, resilient organizations are able to navigate challenges, adapt to change, and achieve long-term success by creating a work environment that fosters collaboration, continuous learning, and employee well-being. By developing these characteristics, leaders can build organizations that are resilient, agile, and able to thrive in today's fast-changing business landscape.

Community Resilience: What does resilience look like at the cultural or society development level?

Resilience at the cultural or societal development level refers to the ability of a community or society to withstand and recover from adverse events or shocks. It can be seen in various aspects of a society, such as its social, economic, political, and environmental systems.

Cultural or Societal resilience might look like:

Social resilience: A society with strong social networks and support systems is more resilient to adverse events such as natural disasters, economic downturns, or pandemics. Social resilience can manifest in the form of community organizations, volunteer groups, and other networks that help individuals and families during times of crisis.

Economic resilience: A resilient society has a diversified economy that can adapt to changing circumstances. This means that if one industry or sector is hit hard by a crisis, other sectors can step up and help keep the economy afloat. Additionally, a resilient economy has a strong safety net to support individuals and businesses during difficult times.

Political resilience: A resilient society has strong institutions and governance structures that can adapt to changing circumstances. This means that during times of crisis, political leaders can work together to make difficult decisions and implement policies that benefit the entire society. Additionally, a resilient society has mechanisms in place to ensure that power is distributed fairly and transparently.

Environmental resilience: A resilient society is able to adapt to and mitigate the impacts of environmental crises such as climate change, natural disasters, and resource depletion. This can manifest in the form of sustainable land use practices, renewable energy sources, and resilient infrastructure that can withstand extreme weather events.

Overall, resilience at the cultural or societal development level is about building strong and adaptive systems that can withstand and recover from shocks, while also promoting long-term sustainability and well-being for all members of society.

Resilience Summary at Development Levels: Individuals, Leaders, Leadership, Organizations, Community

1. Individuals
Resilient individuals are easy-going, i.e., agreeable, recognized for rising to meet challenges and demonstrating resilient behaviors such as self-efficacy, self-awareness, and reflection. Resilient individuals exhibit confidence and compassion, i.e., empathy with the desire to help or improve things. They contribute positive emotional contagion in the form of optimism and hope. Resilient individuals possess intact protective factors demonstrated by strong relationships and positive coping mechanisms, such as mindfulness, meditation and exercise and prayer and music.
Resilient individuals are open-minded and adaptable; they may embrace change with little to no resistance. They are conscientious, socially minded, proactive, and exhibit a strong sense of self. Resilient individuals possess positive coping skills and practice self-care.

2. Leaders
Resilient leaders embody the characteristics of resilient individuals and apply those strengths to influencing resilient behaviors in others. Resilient leaders may work outside of their own comfort zones in order to adjust their leadership styles and approaches to meet organizational needs. They

accept that being human means accepting imperfection as an inevitability that can be corrected through development of protective factors. Resilient leaders understand that failures are just as important, if not more so, than successes for the lessons and opportunities for correction gained from them.

Resilient leaders possess the capability to guide and inspire others through times of uncertainty and fear with confidence and compassion. They build trust and loyalty by making ethical decisions, promoting accountability and ensuring the basic needs and safety of stakeholders. They are skilled communicators and committed to social and situational awareness for recognizing physical, environmental, and behavioral vulnerabilities and providing interventions. They understand the importance of developing resilient protective factors and coping mechanisms for increasing stakeholders' resistance to the potential psychosocial impact of crises and disasters. Resilient leaders represent an opportunity to strengthen human- and social-capital through vicarious learning and positive role-modeling behaviors.

Resilient leaders are skilled in Goleman's (2000) four capabilities of emotional intelligence: self-awareness, self-management, social awareness, and social skill, that represent the process of recognizing one's own perceptions about self and others and how those perceptions influence behavior in the world around them.

Self-awareness represents the ability to recognize and understand the following: (1) one's own emotions and how self-behavior impacts the world around them, i.e., emotional self-awareness, (2) one's own strengths and weaknesses, i.e., accurate self-assessment, and (3) the strength of confidence in one's self, i.e., self-confidence.

Self-management includes: (1) self-control of one's own emotions and behaviors, (2) trustworthiness represented by honesty and integrity, (3) conscientious management of self and responsibilities, (4) the ability to overcome obstacles and adapt to change, (5) the focus on internal excellence, i.e., achievement orientation, and (6) the readiness to embrace adversity as an opportunity.

Social awareness is the combination of sensing the emotions, perspectives, and needs of individuals.

Social skills cover the common leadership skills of vision, influence and change agents, building up others, relationship-building, communication, collaboration, and conflict management.

Resilient leaders use these concepts to critically assess disruptions to determine needs, capabilities, and potential short-term and long-term impacts, and provide meaning to the organization's vision for moving forward. They understand the value of internal and external relationships, such as patient care teams and community partnerships, respectively. They encourage collaborative processes for sharing information, decision-making, and preparedness planning.

Resilient leaders prepare their organizations to meet such capability needs related to crises and disasters by planning ahead and practicing for the unexpected so that if or when they do occur, response will be swift and confident. This includes applying principles in crisis management and high-reliability organizations to educate others, incorporate stakeholders and community partners in practice response, look for vulnerabilities, assess performance against outcomes, process feedback, design and redesign systems and procedures, and effectively implement the changes. Resilient leaders have the capability to guide and inspire others through times of uncertainty with confidence and compassion.

3. Leadership

Resilient leadership is a balancing act of contradictions: the known with the unknown, strength with vulnerability, agency with communion, innovation with preparedness, and a clear vision with flexibility. Resilient leadership represents tangible and intangible means for motivating and guiding others through challenges to reach an outcome of strength. It is deeply rooted in emotional intelligence and the connectedness of relationships. Resilient leadership is the catalyst for inspiring others to exceed personal expectations and is essential for developing cultures of resilience and safety.

When challenges arise, resilient leadership provides the support and flexibility for improvisation from a collective of talents, skills, and knowledge in order to respond to emerging needs and adapt to embrace the changes that such disruptions may bring. It represents a process for empowering stakeholders' resilience capabilities while sustaining current goals and rising to meet market changes and evolving technologies.

4. Organizations

Resilient organizations develop cultures of resilience and safety that embrace continuous learning and adaptive behaviors. They have a preoccupation with failure in that they are driven to reduce errors as much as possible and apply high-reliability organization theory to their habits and processes for continuous assessment and improvement. They are comprised of a workforce that is continuously trained and included in assessments and planning. Feedback, assessment, training, and practice are hallmarks of resilient organizations. Resilient organizations are in compliance with laws and regulations; they have processes and procedures in place to respond appropriately and effectively to disruptions of all types.

Over the past century, great strides have been made in deciphering the motivations behind resilient human behaviors and developing leadership theories. Leadership and behavioral theories were discussed to assess their application to resilience. Four leadership theories appeared to be of the most significance: (1) transformational/transaction leadership, (2) servant leadership, (3) authentic leadership, (4) crisis leadership.

Study of behavioral theories revealed five human capabilities for processing information into perceptions and memories: symbolizing, forethought, observational, self-regulatory, and self-reflective. Human perceptions stood out as having significant bearing on resilience capabilities. Perceptions of particular relevance were discussed in relation to their risks and opportunities for interventions: self-efficacy, emotional contagion, confidence, expectancy, social supports, and control. High-reliability organizations also create safe and resilient work environments.

Leaders are individuals first. Individuals can learn vicarious resilience from leaders who have optimistic mindsets, healthy coping mechanisms, supportive relationships, and a strong sense of self. Self-efficacy and emotional intelligence are also essential areas for development. In order for leaders to be resilient, they need to understand human behavior, starting with their own. Training in psychological first aid and cognitive theories, including development of the five human capabilities, may provide them with the empathetic awareness they need to anticipate people's needs and situations. Resilience requires a preparedness mindset and critical thinking skills that could be further strengthened through crisis management and preparedness education.

Resilient leadership is a modern term for the rising global needs to adapt and recover after significant disruptions; but it is not a new concept. Leaders who can recognize individual, social, and organizational risks and apply interventions to preserve and develop protective factors can fortify the overall resilience of an organization. Resilience represents a choice to reintegrate fully by accepting and adapting to change created by adversity with hope and optimism. Organizational resilience is built from the individual outward, and in turn, as more and more organizations build resilience, societal or cultural resilience is strengthened.

5. Community

Community resilience at the cultural or societal development level involves a society's ability to withstand and recover from adverse events. It encompasses several key aspects:

Social Resilience involves the presence of strong social networks and support systems within the community. It is exemplified by community organizations, volunteer groups, and networks that come to the aid of individuals and families during times of crisis.

Economic Resilience allows a society to maintain a diversified economy that can adapt to changing circumstances. In the face of crises, various sectors can support each other, and there are robust safety nets to assist individuals and businesses during difficult times.

Political Resilience solidifies strong institutions and governance structures capable of adapting to evolving situations. This includes political leaders working together to make challenging decisions during crises and mechanisms ensuring equitable and transparent power distribution.

Environmental Resilience involves a society's capacity to adapt to and mitigate the impacts of environmental crises like climate change, natural disasters, and resource depletion. This is demonstrated through sustainable land use practices, the use of renewable energy sources, and the construction of resilient infrastructure.

Moreover, cultural and societal resilience involves establishing robust, adaptable systems that can withstand shocks while also promoting long-term sustainability and well-being for all members of society.

Chapter 3
The Key Model - Expanding Resilient Leadership

Regardless of the century or triggering event, five common themes arose from the research: identification of a disruption, a need (innate or learned) for survival, an action or reaction to the disruption, knowledge gained from the experience, and the degree of strength gained or lost by the outcome.

The Resilience Leadership Model

Disruption	Survival Instinct	Action / Reaction	Knowledge	Strength
(Event)	(Internalize)	(Response)	(Learning)	(Experience)
Something Happened	Process What Happened	Respond Physically or Verbally	Examine Outcomes	New Normal

1. Disruption= [EVENT]
2. Survival Instinct= [INTERNALIZE]
3. Action/Reaction= [RESPONSE]
4. Knowledge= [LEARNING]
5. Strength= [EXPERIENCE]

Disruption

- Insignificant easily surmountable
- Significant: Emergency, Crisis, Disaster
- Time-sensitive, potential for escalation

Five Basic Human Capabilities:

1. Symbolizing
2. Forethought
3. Observation
4. Self-regulation
5. Self-reflection

These help to identify:
- the disruption
- degree of severity
- estimate impact
- next steps

Opportunity:

1. Growth and development, tracking needed
2. Process improvement
3. Root cause analysis

Leadership Application:

Apply knowledge, skills, and abilities to discern degree of disruption to health and life safety, business continuity, and social and material resources.

1. Disruption

Disruptions occur when a disturbance interrupts the normal course or continuation of [an] activity or process. It is the disturbance - defined as an interruption of a state of peace, quiet, or calm...an interference with or...departure from a norm or standard...an impairment in form, function, or activity- that triggers the disruption. The degree of disruption is generally interpreted as significant or insignificant which, in turn, triggers the instinctual or learned need for survival. Perceptions are highly individualized, meaning that the perceived degree of disruption and its psychological impact will vary by individual and organization.

Depending upon severity, disruptions may be significant or merely mild annoyances that do not detract from one's ability to respond, recover, and adapt, such as stubbing a toe. Disruptions of significance are referred to as emergencies, crises, or disasters. Emergencies are disruptions that require immediate response to protect life or property. An emergency is usually something to which an adaptation is quickly made and the issue resolved.

When an emergency evolves to reach a critical decision-making point in which there is a distinct possibility of a highly undesirable outcome, it has become a crisis. Crises are disruptions with a potential psychosocial impact that require critical thinking and imply a time-pressured change from normal practices. Supply chain disruptions can exemplify crises. When a strain of coronavirus later identified as severe acute respiratory syndrome (SARS) broke out in Taiwan in 2003, hospital administrators recognized the peril and ordered personal protective equipment from not one, but at least six suppliers to ensure a constant supply. In this instance, preventing supply chain disruption contributed to the overall success of a hospital that would eventually have the third highest number of SARS cases in the country.

Crises escalate into disasters when needs exceed resources and capacities, such as a natural catastrophe, technological accident, or human-caused event that has resulted in severe property damage, deaths, and/or multiple injuries. When Hurricane Katrina hit states along the Gulf of Mexico coastline in 2005, it destroyed five hospitals, including the 550-bed Charity Hospital and the 400-bed Veterans Administration Hospital. More than one million people across three states rushed to flee the storm. Of those who remained in New Orleans, Louisiana, were physicians and nurses at Charity Hospital and surrounding healthcare facilities in New Orleans who had to work under unbelievable conditions, with no electricity or water, in buildings reaching 35 degrees Celsius and 100% humidity for five days before relief began to arrive. The lessons learned from this natural disaster have reshaped the world in terms of healthcare preparedness and disaster-related legislation.

Disruption- How does disruption impact the development of resilience?

Disruptions happen every day, but they are not always crises or disasters. Resilient leaders combine instincts, learned knowledge, and experiences to make sense of and provide meaning to disruptions. The initial disturbance occurs quickly and, in those minutes, resilient leaders begin to process the situation through five basic human capabilities: (1) symbolizing, (2) forethought, (3) observation, (4) self-regulatory, and (5) self-reflection in order to identify the disruption, discern the degree of severity, and estimate its impact on physical and emotional health and safety, business continuity, and human, social, and material resources. This event-focused stage prompts resilient leaders to look ahead and estimate what conditions may be in a few hours, in a few days, in a month, and so forth to predict present, short-term, and long-term needs, capabilities, and constraints.

Disruption can actually be a catalyst for the development of resilience in individuals and teams. When disruptions occur, they can cause significant challenges and uncertainty, which can be overwhelming for individuals and teams. However, by overcoming these challenges, individuals and teams can develop the resilience needed to bounce back and adapt to future disruptions.

Disruption can force individuals and teams to think creatively and outside of the box, which can lead to new ideas and solutions. It can also highlight areas where improvements are needed, which can ultimately strengthen the team and organization. Disruption can also create opportunities for growth and development, both personally and professionally.

On the other hand, if disruptions are not handled well, they can lead to negative outcomes such as increased stress, burnout, and decreased morale.

Therefore, it is important for individuals and teams to have the skills, knowledge, and resources needed to manage disruptions effectively.

Developing resilience requires intentional effort and practice, and it can be enhanced through training and support. When individuals and teams are equipped with the tools to handle disruptions, they are more likely to emerge stronger and more capable than before. In this way, disruption can be a valuable opportunity for growth and development, both for individuals and organizations as a whole.

Survival Instinct

• **Sense of urgency, motivation**
1. Instinctual – fight or flight
2. Learned

• **Crisis Leadership**
1. Command/leadership
2. Trust
3. Shared goals

• **Opportunity**
1. Harness short-term goals

• **Leadership application**
1. Transformational leadership
2. Innovation and growth opportunities
3. Balance short-term view with long-term/big picture view and plans

2. Survival Instinct

The act of survival was present long before recorded history and is evidenced by every living being in the world today. Survival is driven by natural and learned instincts toward life and recovery. The outcome of survival is commonly referred to as survival of the fittest - a term created by

Herbert Spencer in response to Charles Darwin's research as a naturalist in the mid-1800s. However, Darwin felt there was a term better suited for the variables involved in survival and favored Thomas Malthus's description, "struggle for existence." When compared to resilience, the latter term is more accurate for this discussion.

The desire to survive is not enough. Generally speaking, survival requires some form of motivational energy such as an emotional response (reaction) and recognition or learning (knowledge) in order to be achieved.

Survival Instinct - How does the survival instinct impact the development of resilience?

Resilient leaders contribute to an organization's overall survival by maintaining business continuity and applying principles in crisis management to proactively prepare for, respond to, mitigate, cope with, and recover from potential disasters. However, the initial state of survival described the motivational need to survive. In this regard, resilient leaders should apply a plethora of principles in leadership, motivation, and change theories to instill trust and establish a sense of urgency to move forward with a clear vision of a shared goal.

The survival instinct can play a crucial role in the development of resilience. The survival instinct is an innate biological drive that humans and many animals possess to protect themselves and stay alive in threatening situations. When faced with adversity, the survival instinct can trigger the body's "fight or flight" response, which can help individuals to cope with the stress and overcome the challenges they face.

The survival instinct can motivate individuals to persist in the face of adversity and to keep moving forward, even when the odds are stacked against them. This persistence can be a key factor in the development of resilience, as individuals learn to adapt to new situations and overcome obstacles through sheer force of will. However, the survival instinct can also have negative consequences if not managed properly. When individuals become too focused on survival, they may become overly cautious or risk-averse, which can limit their ability to take risks and innovate. In addition, the survival instinct can lead to a narrow focus on short-term goals, which can prevent individuals from seeing the bigger picture and planning for the future.

Therefore, while the survival instinct can be a powerful tool in developing resilience, it is important to balance it with a broader perspective and a long-term outlook. Individuals and teams who are able to harness the survival instinct and use it to drive innovation and growth are more likely to develop the resilience needed to succeed in today's rapidly changing business environment.

Action/Reaction

- Proactive
1. Prevention – focused: planning, practice, drills

- Reactive
1. Unexpected, uncertain path for response
2. Emotional: paralyzed decision-making, fear, psychosocial distress

- Disaster Preparedness Plan – Key Element

- Resilient Leader
1. Act with courage
2. Make decisions based on current knowledge
3. Plan, train, practice, gather feedback (on-going)
4. Learn, grow, and develop

- Value Proactive Responses Over Reactive Responses
   Leadership application – Proactive Responses
1. Take action
2. Seek solutions
3. Develop coping strategies

Yields:
- a sense of control
- focus on what they "can do"

3. Action/Reaction

Response to a disruption is produced by actions and reactions. Actions are proactive or planned responses and reactions are emotional responses. The grief and mourning that follows the shock of loss and destruction are examples of emotional responses. Response may seem automatic or intuitive, such as when a life is in danger and strangers spontaneously gather to use their strengths and expertise toward the common goal of getting the person to safety. Intuitive responses are based in cognitive learning and are the mind's way of guiding individuals toward resilience. An action may also be a prepared response to a threshold of change, such as developing a disaster preparedness plan that identifies trigger criteria for coordinating the evacuation of patients from a long-term care facility. In the theme of resilience, actions and reactions may be intuitive, learned, or a combination of both.

Action/Reaction - How does action and reaction impact the development of resilience?

Resilient leaders act with courage to prioritize needs amid rapidly changing conditions and make decisions with imperfect information while navigating the shifting needs and perspectives of stakeholders in order to instill trust in and viability of the organization. They understand that reactions stem from the uncertainties of being unprepared and underprepared to meet adversities. Thus, they have a preoccupation with preparedness activities such as planning, training, practice, and immediate feedback in order to ensure positive self-efficacy in themselves and their organizations.

Action and reaction can play a significant role in the development of resilience. When faced with adversity, individuals and teams can choose to react in different ways. Reactive responses might include feelings of anger, frustration, or despair, or behaviors like avoidance, blame, or giving up. However, these reactive responses can be detrimental to the development of resilience, as they often lead to a sense of helplessness and a lack of control over the situation.

On the other hand, proactive responses can be much more beneficial for the development of resilience. Proactive responses involve taking action, seeking out solutions, and developing coping strategies to overcome the challenges at hand. This proactive approach can help individuals and teams to regain a sense of control over the situation and to focus on what they can do, rather than what they can't.

Action and reaction can also impact the development of resilience in terms of learning and growth. When individuals and teams take proactive steps to overcome adversity, they can learn from their experiences and develop new skills and competencies. This can lead to greater confidence and resilience in the face of future challenges. However, it is important to note that taking action and being proactive does not mean that individuals and teams need to have all the answers or be able to solve every problem on their own. Developing resilience also involves recognizing when to seek help and support from others, whether it be from colleagues, friends, or professional resources.

In summary, action and reaction can have a significant impact on the development of resilience. Proactive responses that focus on taking action, seeking solutions, and learning from experiences can help individuals and teams to overcome adversity and develop greater resilience.

Knowledge

- Experiential

- Learned
1. Vicarious observation
2. Emotional contagion

- Resilient Leaders Apply
1. Lessons learned from prior events
2. Use preparedness training
3. Practice preparedness drills

- Resilient Leaders Display
1. Optimism
2. Calm in the face of chaos
3. Conscientious response
4. Preparedness behavior

- Resilient Leaders Have Coping Strategies
1. Mindfulness
2. Exercise
3. Social supports

- Leadership Application
1. Reflection (debrief)
2. Sense making
3. Lessons learned, feedback

- Vicarious Resilience
1. Role-modeling, positive resilience behavior
2. Mentoring and coaching
3. Communicating shared experiences

4. Knowledge

Knowledge is a result of action, experiential or didactic. It is a culmination of trial and errors, what worked and what did not. Knowledge was a great influencer of resilience evolution. For example, the twentieth century gave rise to industrialization and with it came industrial accidents and disasters. In 1979, experiences and lessons learned from "inefficient and fragmented" response efforts to contain and mitigate the partial nuclear core meltdown at Three Mile Island in Pennsylvania reinforced the need for a coordinated emergency management agency. This disaster contributed to President Jimmy Carter creating the Federal Emergency Management Agency that is now simply referred to as FEMA.

Knowledge - How does knowledge impact the development of resilience?

Resilient leaders apply lessons learned from previous crises, disasters, and preparedness training to continuously prepare, plan, and practice in order to elevate human and social capital resilience capabilities. They value immediate feedback and periods of reflection as sense-making opportunities to understand contexts, lessons learned, and successes. As inherent role-models, resilient leaders inspire vicarious resilience in others by projecting optimism, calm in the face of chaos, conscientious response, and preparedness behaviors. Resilient leaders understand the complexities of human behavior and apply cognitive theories to invention processes and concepts of emotional intelligence to support self-awareness, social awareness, and reflection.

Knowledge can play a crucial role in the development of resilience. When individuals and teams have knowledge about the challenges they face, they are better equipped to respond to those challenges in a proactive and effective way.

This knowledge, which can take various forms, including a clear understanding of the nature and scope of the challenges, can assist individuals and teams in developing effective strategies for addressing them. This may involve gathering information about the situation, conducting research, or consulting with experts or colleagues.

Individuals and teams who have knowledge of effective coping strategies are better equipped to manage stress and adversity. Coping strategies may include mindfulness practices, exercise, social support, or other forms of self-care. Knowing where to turn for help and support can be critical in times of adversity. This may include knowledge of organizational resources like employee assistance programs, health and wellness services, and community resources, such as counseling services or support groups. Learning from past experiences can also be a valuable source of knowledge for developing resilience. Reflecting on past successes and failures can help individuals and teams to identify what works and what doesn't, and to develop strategies for coping with future challenges.

By developing knowledge in these areas, individuals and teams can become more resilient and better able to adapt to changing circumstances. However, it is important to note that knowledge alone is not sufficient for developing resilience. It must be combined with action and a proactive approach in order to be effective.

Strength

Outcome, degree of reintegration
1. Reintegrate fully: adapt to and embrace the "new normal"
2. Reintegrate without change: maintain "status quo"
3. Reintegrate with loss: failure to adapt "stagnate"
4. Capacity to overcome the next significant disruption

Strength is found within
1. Teams, organizations and communities that are resilient
2. Traits, skills, and capabilities that first beings with the individual
3. Mental strength
   • Positive mindset
   • Optimistic
   • Manage stress and emotions
   • Self-confidence
   • Learn from failure

Leadership Appreciation
1. Establish a culture of resilience and culture of safety with focus on:
2. Use preparedness training
3. Practice preparedness drills
   • Well-being – physical and emotional
   • Flexibility – adaptable
   • Preparedness
   • Continuity
   • Recovery

5. Strength

Strength as resilience is the outcome of action and knowledge. Strength is gained by leveraging positive attitudes and knowledge from previous experiences to bolster protective factors for resilience. The degree of outcome determines the level of strength achieved. For instance, resisting change in the aftermath of disasters may stagnate an organization's recovery. Conversely, organizations that embrace innovation and adapt to what is commonly referred to as the 'new normal' may exceed simple survival and thrive beyond expectations. In short, strength is achieved by accepting and embracing change.

In the early 1900s, Gwin (1930) observed self-rehabilitation as a strength. This strength was exemplified when communities that had lost major crops to extensive flooding set aside societal and cultural differences. Instead, they focused on increasing food stability with the cultivation of corn and alfalfa in a region that was previously known for growing cotton. By the 1960s, educators were struggling to produce positive outcomes in students who were at socio-economic and psychological risk. So, they began pushing for collaboration from external forces within their communities. They realized the task of improving service delivery, reducing student risks, and increasing students' strength of outcomes could not be achieved alone. In 2020, the Centers for Medicare & Medicaid Services response during the COVID-19 pandemic embraced technological change. It removed reimbursement and licensing barriers in telemedicine to accommodate the needs of patients to be seen and providers to minimize everyone's exposure to COVID-19. These examples represent the innovative thinking and collaboration that are now common hallmarks of resilience and leadership.

The five aforementioned components of resilience are integral to the understanding of how disruptions are processed by human behaviors. This knowledge may be used to identify strengths and weaknesses for resilience in individuals and organizations. It is also a building block for resilience models which has been developed and shared in this book.

Strength - How does mental strength impact the development of resilience?

Strength is demonstrated by what resilience looks like in individuals, leaders, leadership, and organizations. As previously discussed, resilience begins with the capabilities of individuals and expands to include organizations. Thus, strength will be discussed as the traits, skills, and capabilities identified earlier in behavioral and leadership theories that build from the individual outward.

Mental strength can play a significant role in the development of resilience. Mental strength refers to the ability to maintain a positive and proactive mindset in the face of adversity, and to cope with stress and challenges in a healthy and effective way. When individuals and teams have mental strength, they are better able to persevere in the face of difficulty, adapt to changing circumstances, and bounce back from setbacks.

Some of the ways in which mental strength can impact the development of resilience include developing a positive mindset. Mental strength involves developing a positive and optimistic outlook, even in the face of adversity. This positive mindset can help individuals and teams to maintain their motivation and focus, and to stay resilient in the face of challenges.

Mental strength also involves building self-confidence and self-efficacy, which can help individuals and teams to believe in their ability to overcome challenges and succeed in the face of adversity. Individuals and teams with mental strength are better able to cope with stress and anxiety, and to manage their emotions in a healthy and productive way. This can help to reduce the negative impact of stress on resilience and increase the ability to stay focused on the task at hand. Mental strength also involves the ability to learn from failure and setbacks, and to use these experiences as opportunities for growth and development. This can help individuals and teams to develop greater resilience and to bounce back more quickly from future challenges. Mental strength can have a significant impact on the development of resilience by: (1) helping individuals and teams to maintain a positive and proactive mindset, (2) build self-confidence, (3) cope with stress and anxiety, and (4) learn from failure. Developing mental strength requires ongoing effort and practice but can lead to greater resilience and success in the face of adversity.

Chapter 4
Resilient Leadership Styles

Stepping into Resilience

Resilience refers to an individual's ability to adapt and recover from challenging or stressful situations. It is the capacity to bounce back from adversity, trauma, or stressors in a healthy way. Resilience is not something that people are born with; it is a skill that can be developed and strengthened through practice.

Who can develop resilience? Anyone, regardless of age, background, or life experience, can develop resilience. It is a skill that can be developed at any time in one's life.

What is resilience? It is the ability to cope with life's difficulties and adapt to changing circumstances. Resilience involves the development of coping skills, positive attitudes, and social support networks.

When can resilience be developed? Resilience can be developed at any time, but it is particularly important to develop resilience before experiencing a crisis or adversity. Developing resilience skills can help individuals better cope with and recover from challenging situations.

Where can resilience be developed? Resilience can be developed in various settings, including schools, workplaces, and communities. It can also be developed through personal practices such as mindfulness, positive self-talk, and building positive relationships.

Why is resilience important? Resilience is important because it helps individuals to better cope with and recover from stressful situations, such as job loss, illness, or relationship difficulties. It also promotes mental health and well-being, which can improve overall quality of life.

How can resilience be developed? Resilience can be developed through a variety of practices, including developing coping skills, building positive relationships, practicing mindfulness and self-compassion, and seeking support from others. Building resilience takes time, effort, and practice, but it is a worthwhile investment in one's overall health and well-being.

The Underpinnings of Resilient Leadership

Resilience and leadership are closely connected, as leaders who demonstrate resilience are better equipped to navigate challenges and inspire others to do the same. Leaders who model resilience can help their team members to develop this skill, creating a more adaptive and resilient organization. Resilient leaders are able to persevere in the face of adversity, maintain a positive outlook, and learn from their experiences. They are also more likely to remain calm and focused on difficult situations, which can help them to make better decisions and communicate effectively with their team. Overall, resilience is an essential skill for effective leadership, and leaders who prioritize their own resilience and that of their team members can create a more successful and resilient organization.

1. Transformational Leadership

Transformational leadership is a leadership style in which the leader inspires and motivates their followers to achieve their goals and to work towards a shared vision. Transformational leaders empower their followers by helping them develop their skills, promoting creativity, and providing support and recognition for their achievements. They also focus on creating a positive organizational culture that fosters innovation, growth, and development.

Transformational leadership is largely known through the contributions of Bernard Bass's to James MacGregor Burns's earlier research whereby they suggest that followers and leaders inspire each other to achieve positive change and growth. Transformational leaders are charismatic, inspire loyalty and respect, and motivate followers to achieve change. The factors attributed to Bass (1985) that distinguish transformational leadership have become known as intellectual stimulation, individualized consideration, inspirational motivation, and idealized influence. Leaders who inspire creative thinking and support innovation are utilizing intellectual stimulation. Encouraging the development of others through mentorships and coaching are forms of individualized consideration. Inspirational motivation may be achieved through clear communication of a shared vision. Role-modeling behavior is representative of idealized influence.

A large part of transformational leadership is influencing others to want to change and adapt. Transformational leaders inspire connections and greater performance by helping followers understand the importance of change and how they can contribute to it, placing the interests of followers and the organization ahead of their own, and showing enthusiasm toward meeting followers' esteem and self-actualization needs.

Transactional leadership theory is characterized by a mutually beneficial relationship between leaders and followers. Transactional leaders are performance-oriented, provide clear role and task expectations; however, unlike the emotional connection that accompanies authentic, servant, and transformational leaders, perceptions of transactional leaders are based on their achievement successes and failures. Whereas transactional leadership as reciprocal exchanges between leaders and followers, meaning that benefits are gained on both sides. Transactional leadership uses contingency rewards to motivate others' performance and management by exception to micromanaging others. When used constructively, management by exception allows leaders to recognize and correct specific behaviors which require attention and has been shown to improve perceptions and outcomes. However, it can also contribute to over-management and struggles over sense of agency, i.e., control.

When crises or disasters occur, existing responsibilities may be shifted but the resilient leader understands the importance of meeting current service needs while also adapting to the rapidly changing environment brought on by adversity. Leaders today are facing situations in which they have no experience from which to draw knowledge. To meet the needs of unfamiliar crises with resilience, leaders will have to move between transformational and transactional leadership styles.

2. Servant Leadership
Servant leadership is a leadership philosophy in which the leader puts the needs of their followers first and serves them, rather than the other way around. Servant leaders prioritize the development and well-being of their followers, and they strive to create a culture of trust, collaboration, and

empowerment. They are often described as humble, empathetic, and compassionate.

Servant leadership is also suggested to overlap with rising themes in resilient leadership. The theory of servant leadership draws from the mindset of stewardship and wanting others to succeed above personal gains and desires. Servant leaders focus on the psychological needs and empowerment of others which inspires higher engagement and performance by their followers. Researchers found servant leaders to be humble, compassionate, service-oriented, open-minded, and socially sensitive with a willingness to learn and admit mistakes. Servant leaders are altruistic stewards who are interested in followers as individuals which promotes a sense of personal familiarity and trust.

Servant leaders conceptualize transparency in being human that is relatable and inspiring to others and that their focus on promoting the well-being of others positions them well to support rising themes in resilient leadership. Servant leaders' genuine interest in followers' well-being and development may bolster followers' attitudes and resilience through emotional contagion, i.e., vicarious influence and recommends developing emotional intelligence competency and implementing plans for education, career, and individual development to promote resilience in servant leaders.

3. Authentic Leadership

Authentic leadership is a leadership style that emphasizes the leader's genuineness, transparency, and ethical conduct. Authentic leaders are self-aware and have a strong sense of their values and beliefs. They lead by example and strive to create an environment in which others feel safe to be themselves and express their opinions. Authentic leaders also value the importance of building relationships based on trust and respect.

Authentic leadership is rooted in the notion that transparency and being true to one's self exudes a sense of realness that is admired among followers.

Authentic leaders are thought to instill trust in others by making them feel safe. They are associated with integrity, hope, optimism, and inspiring respect and loyalty from others. Self-awareness regarding their own strengths, weaknesses, morals, and beliefs is the "cornerstone of authentic leadership." Additional factors of authentic leadership include self-regulation, balanced processing, and relational transparency. Authentic leaders may inspire higher moral and ethical standards in others. These components of authentic leadership are suggested to overlap with rising themes in resilient leadership. Research further suggests that the transparent and ethical influence of authentic leadership would promote resilience by contributing a sense of morality to decision-making. The understanding of authentic leadership may be strengthened by engaging in "risk-taking, vulnerability, and self-reflection."

4. Crisis Leadership
Crisis leadership is a leadership style that is focused on managing and leading organizations through challenging and uncertain times. Crisis leaders must be decisive, adaptable, and skilled at managing risks and making difficult decisions. They must also be able to communicate effectively, provide clear direction, and inspire confidence and trust in their

These four leadership styles are part of what makes a Resilient Leader.

followers. Crisis leaders often work under intense pressure and must be able to maintain their composure and focus on the task at hand.

In the 1980s, Ian Mitroff introduced the concept of crisis management theory in response to organizational crises and large-scale industrial disasters, such as the near meltdown of the Three Mile Island Nuclear Power Plant's reactor core. The penultimate goal of crisis management is to prevent, control, and recover from disruptions precipitated by people, organizational structures, economics, and/or technology that cause extensive damage to human life and natural and social environments. Mitroff proposed four phases of crisis management: (1) detection, (2) crisis, (3) repair, and (4) assessment, that can be used proactively to prevent, prepare, and learn or reactively to cope and recover.

Key Takeaway

While all four leadership styles share some common traits, they differ in their focus, priorities, and characteristics. Transformational leadership emphasizes vision, empowerment, and positive culture. Servant leadership prioritizes followers' needs and well-being. Authentic leadership emphasizes ethical conduct and transparency. Crisis leadership focuses on managing challenging situations effectively.

Resilient Leadership - A Culmination of Leadership Theories

How do these leadership styles lead to resilient leadership?

All four leadership styles - Transformational, Servant, Authentic, and Crisis - can contribute to building resilience in organizations and teams.

1. **Transformational leaders** can help to build resilience by creating a positive and supportive organizational culture that encourages innovation and growth. By empowering their followers and promoting creativity, they can help to develop new solutions and ideas that enable organizations to adapt to changing circumstances.

Transformational leadership is a crucial component of the journey towards resilient leadership. Transformational leaders inspire and motivate their teams to achieve high levels of performance, adapt to change, and navigate challenges effectively. Here's how transformational leadership contributes to resilience:

Vision and direction: Transformational leaders provide a compelling vision and clear direction for the organization. They articulate a future state and communicate the purpose and goals in a way that inspires and motivates employees. A well-defined vision helps employees understand the organization's purpose, align their efforts, and maintain focus during challenging times. This clarity of direction enhances the organization's resilience by providing a guiding framework for decision-making and actions.

Inspirational motivation: Transformational leaders inspire and motivate their teams by setting high expectations, fostering enthusiasm, and creating a sense of purpose. They communicate optimism, passion, and confidence, even in the face of adversity. This inspirational motivation encourages employees to persevere, overcome obstacles, and embrace change. By instilling a resilient mindset, transformational leaders help individuals and the organization bounce back from setbacks and maintain a positive outlook.

Individualized support: Transformational leaders provide individualized support and mentorship to their team members. They understand the strengths, weaknesses, and aspirations of their employees and provide guidance and development opportunities accordingly. By recognizing and leveraging individual talents, transformational leaders empower employees to contribute their best, build confidence, and develop resilience. This personalized support enhances employee engagement and fosters a sense of ownership and commitment to the organization's success.

Intellectual stimulation: Transformational leaders promote intellectual stimulation by encouraging critical thinking, creativity, and innovation. They challenge assumptions, stimulate curiosity, and foster a learning culture within the organization. This intellectual stimulation enables employees to think creatively, explore new possibilities, and adapt to changing circumstances. By promoting a growth mindset and encouraging the exploration of alternative solutions, transformational leaders enhance the organization's resilience by enabling adaptive thinking and problem-solving.

Building relationships and collaboration: Transformational leaders prioritize building strong relationships and fostering collaboration among team members. They promote open communication, active listening, and respect for diverse perspectives. These relationship-building efforts create a supportive and cohesive work environment that encourages teamwork, trust, and effective collaboration. Strong relationships and collaboration enhance resilience by enabling effective communication, knowledge sharing, and collective problem-solving during times of uncertainty or crisis.

Empowering others: Transformational leaders empower their employees by delegating authority, encouraging autonomy, and fostering a sense of ownership. They trust their team members and provide them with the necessary resources and decision-making power to accomplish their goals. Empowering employees enhances their confidence, autonomy, and accountability. This empowerment leads to greater resilience as employees feel empowered to take initiative, make informed decisions, and adapt to changing circumstances.

2. **Servant leaders** can build resilience by focusing on the well-being of their followers. By prioritizing the development and support of their followers, they can help to create a culture of trust, collaboration, and empowerment. This can lead to increased resilience by fostering a sense of community and

shared purpose, and by enabling individuals to support each other during challenging times.

Servant leadership is an essential component of the journey towards resilient leadership. Servant leaders prioritize the needs of their team members, empower them, and foster a supportive work environment. Here's how servant leadership contributes to resilience:

Focus on employee well-being: Servant leaders genuinely care about the well-being of their team members. They prioritize creating a supportive work environment where employees feel valued, respected, and psychologically safe. By promoting work-life balance, offering support systems, and addressing individual needs, servant leaders enhance employee well-being. When employees feel supported and their well-being is prioritized, they are better equipped to cope with challenges, bounce back from setbacks, and contribute to organizational resilience.

Empowerment and trust: Servant leaders empower their team members by trusting their abilities and providing them with autonomy and decision-making authority. They delegate responsibility and provide the necessary resources and support for employees to succeed. This empowerment fosters a sense of ownership, accountability, and self-efficacy among employees. Empowered employees are more likely to take initiative, make decisions, and adapt to changing circumstances, contributing to the organization's resilience.

Collaboration and teamwork: Servant leaders promote collaboration and teamwork by creating a culture of trust, open communication, and inclusivity. They facilitate cooperation and encourage the sharing of ideas, knowledge, and expertise among team members. Collaboration enhances resilience by leveraging diverse perspectives, fostering creativity, and enabling effective problem-solving. When employees feel valued and included, they are more likely to work together, support one another, and collectively navigate challenges and uncertainties.

Listening and empathy: Servant leaders are skilled listeners and empathetic individuals. They actively listen to their team members, seeking to understand their perspectives, concerns, and needs. By demonstrating empathy, servant leaders create a supportive environment where employees feel heard, understood, and valued. This fosters trust, builds stronger relationships, and promotes psychological well-being. Empathetic leaders are better equipped to provide the necessary support during challenging times, enabling individuals to cope with adversity and enhancing organizational resilience.

Development and growth: Servant leaders prioritize the development and growth of their team members. They invest in their employees' professional and personal development, provide coaching and mentorship, and create opportunities for learning. By supporting continuous growth, servant leaders enhance employee engagement, satisfaction, and resilience. When employees feel supported in their growth journey, they are more likely to adapt to new challenges, embrace change, and contribute to the organization's resilience through their evolving skills and capabilities.

Ethical and values-based leadership: Servant leaders operate with high ethical standards and uphold organizational values. They lead by example, modeling integrity, fairness, and ethical behavior. This ethical leadership fosters trust and credibility within the organization. Employees who perceive their leaders as ethical and values-driven are more likely to remain committed and resilient, even in the face of challenges or ethical dilemmas.

3. Authentic Leaders can contribute to resilience by fostering transparency, honesty, and ethical conduct. By being open and honest about the challenges and uncertainties faced by the organization, they can help to build trust and encourage a culture of constructive feedback and problem-solving. This can help organizations to respond more effectively to change and to maintain their integrity in challenging situations.

Authentic leadership plays a significant role in the journey towards resilient leadership. Resilient leadership refers to the ability of leaders to navigate and thrive amidst challenges, uncertainties, and setbacks. Authentic leadership, characterized by self-awareness, transparency, and a genuine approach to leading others, contributes to this journey in a variety of ways:

Building trust: Authentic leaders are transparent and genuine in their interactions, which fosters trust among team members. Trust is essential for resilience because it strengthens relationships, encourages open communication, and facilitates collaboration during difficult times. When employees trust their leaders, they are more likely to openly share concerns, seek support, and work together to overcome challenges, enhancing the organization's resilience.

Emotional intelligence: Authentic leaders possess a high degree of emotional intelligence, enabling them to understand and manage their own emotions and those of others. This emotional intelligence allows them to effectively support and empathize with their team members during challenging periods. By recognizing and validating emotions, authentic leaders create a psychologically safe environment where individuals feel supported and can better cope with stress, contributing to the organization's resilience.

Promoting a positive culture: Authentic leaders set the tone for the organization's culture by embodying their values and principles. They create a positive work environment that encourages open communication, learning, and growth. A positive culture promotes resilience by fostering employee engagement, innovation, and adaptability. It also encourages individuals to take calculated risks, learn from failures, and bounce back from setbacks, strengthening the organization's ability to respond to and recover from adversity.

Supporting employee well-being: Authentic leaders prioritize the well-being of their employees, recognizing that their physical and mental health is crucial for resilience. They encourage work-life balance, advocate for manageable workloads, and provide support systems and resources to help employees cope with stress. By prioritizing well-being, authentic leaders contribute to higher employee morale, reduced burnout, and increased resilience within the organization.

Promoting growth and development: Authentic leaders are committed to the growth and development of their team members. They provide opportunities for learning, offer constructive feedback, and support individual career aspirations. By nurturing the growth of employees, authentic leaders foster a learning culture that encourages continuous improvement and adaptability. This focus on growth enables individuals and the organization to develop the skills and capabilities necessary to navigate challenges and seize opportunities, enhancing resilience.

4. Crisis leaders can build resilience by effectively managing challenging and uncertain situations. By providing clear direction and communication, making difficult decisions, and maintaining their composure under pressure, they can inspire confidence and trust in their followers. This can help organizations to weather crises and emerge stronger on the other side. Crisis leadership is a critical component of the journey towards resilient leadership. Resilient leaders are able to effectively navigate and lead their organizations through crises and challenging situations. Here's how crisis leadership contributes to resilience:

Preparedness and planning: Resilient leaders understand the importance of proactive crisis preparedness and planning. They anticipate potential crises, assess risks, and develop robust contingency plans. By having preparedness measures in place, leaders can respond swiftly and effectively during a crisis, minimizing its impact and ensuring the organization can bounce back more quickly.

Clear communication: Crisis leadership involves clear and timely communication with all stakeholders. Resilient leaders provide transparent and accurate information, keeping employees, customers, and other relevant parties informed about the situation, response efforts, and expectations. Effective communication builds trust, reduces uncertainty, and enables coordinated action, which is vital for resilience during crises.

Decisive decision-making: Resilient leaders are capable of making tough decisions in high-pressure situations. They gather information, consult with experts, consider various perspectives, and make timely and informed choices. Decisive decision-making helps to steer the organization through uncertainty and allows for swift action, minimizing the impact of the crisis and enhancing resilience.

Adaptability and agility: Crisis leadership requires adaptability and agility in response to rapidly changing circumstances. Resilient leaders remain flexible and open-minded, willing to adjust strategies and plans as new information emerges. They are proactive in identifying and seizing opportunities that arise during crises, enabling the organization to adapt and recover more effectively.

Emotional intelligence and support: Resilient leaders demonstrate emotional intelligence during crises. They understand and empathize with the emotions of their team members and stakeholders. By providing support and reassurance, resilient leaders help individuals cope with the stress and uncertainty of the crisis. Emotional support fosters resilience by maintaining morale, reducing anxiety, and enabling individuals to focus on problem-solving and recovery.

Learning and growth: Crisis leadership involves a focus on learning and growth. Resilient leaders facilitate post-crisis debriefings and evaluations to identify lessons learned and areas for improvement. They encourage a culture of continuous learning, using the crisis as an opportunity for organizational growth and development. This emphasis on learning and growth strengthens the organization's ability to anticipate and respond to future crises with greater resilience.

Stakeholder collaboration: Resilient leaders recognize the importance of collaborating with stakeholders during a crisis. They foster partnerships with external entities, such as government agencies, industry peers, and community organizations. Collaborative efforts increase the collective capacity to respond and recover from crises, leveraging resources, expertise, and support to enhance resilience.

Key Takeaway

Each of these leadership styles can contribute to resilience in different ways by fostering a positive organizational culture, prioritizing the well-being of followers, promoting transparency and ethical conduct, and effectively managing crises and uncertainty.

Resilient Leadership is built on a strong foundation of Emotional Intelligence

Emotional intelligence (EI) can play a significant role in the development of resilience in leaders and organizations. EI is the ability to recognize, understand, and manage one's own emotions and those of others, and it has been shown to be an important predictor of leadership effectiveness and resilience.

In the context of leadership styles, EI can impact the way in which each style is implemented and the degree to which it contributes to resilience. Here are some examples:

1. Transformational Leadership: Transformational leaders with high EI are able to connect with their followers on an emotional level, inspiring and motivating them to achieve their goals. They are also better able to recognize and respond to the emotions of their followers, providing support and encouragement when needed. This can lead to increased resilience by fostering a sense of shared purpose and commitment.

2. Servant Leadership: Servant leaders with high EI are able to empathize with the needs and emotions of their followers, and they prioritize their well-being accordingly. They are also able to communicate effectively, fostering a sense of trust and collaboration. This can lead to increased resilience by enabling individuals to support each other and work together to overcome challenges.

3. Authentic Leadership: Authentic leaders with high EI are able to recognize and manage their own emotions, which enables them to communicate more effectively and build trust with their followers. They are also able to recognize and respond to the emotions of their followers, providing support and encouragement when needed. This can lead to increased resilience by fostering transparency and open communication.

4. Crisis Leadership: Crisis leaders with high EI are able to remain calm and composed under pressure, making clear and effective decisions in challenging situations. They are also able to recognize and manage the emotions of their followers, providing support and guidance when needed. This can lead to increased resilience by enabling organizations to respond quickly and effectively to crises.

Key Takeaway

Emotional intelligence can impact the way in which each leadership style is implemented and the degree to which it contributes to resilience. Leaders with high EI are able to recognize and manage their own emotions, communicate effectively, and respond to the emotions of their followers, all of which are important factors in building resilience.

Chapter 5
The Development of Resilience

The key elements to developing resilience

Developing resilience is a process that involves a range of strategies and behaviors that help individuals and organizations adapt to and recover from challenging circumstances. While there is no single recipe for building resilience, there are four key elements that are critical to the process.

1. Build and Maintain Strong Relationships

The first key element is the ability to build and maintain strong relationships and social support networks. Research has consistently shown that individuals and organizations with strong social networks are better able to cope with stress and adversity and are more likely to recover from challenging circumstances. This means investing time and energy in building relationships with family, friends, colleagues, and other members of the community.

2. Adapt to Changing Circumstances

The second key element is the ability to adapt to changing circumstances. Resilient individuals and organizations are able to be flexible and adaptable in response to unexpected challenges and opportunities. This means being willing to take calculated risks, experimenting with new approaches, and learning from both success and failure.

3. Positive Thinking and Optimism

The third key element is a focus on positive thinking and optimism. Resilient individuals and organizations are able to maintain a positive outlook and remain hopeful, even in the face of adversity. This means focusing on strengths and opportunities, rather than weaknesses and threats, and looking for ways to reframe challenges as opportunities for growth and development.

4. Prioritize Self-care for Your Physical and Emotional Well-being

The fourth key element is the ability to take care of oneself, both physically and emotionally. Resilient individuals and organizations prioritize self-care, recognizing that taking care of oneself is critical to maintaining the energy, focus, and resilience needed to navigate challenging circumstances. This means making time for rest, exercise, and other forms of self-care, as well as seeking support from mental health professionals when needed.

Overall, developing resilience requires a combination of personal and interpersonal skills, as well as a commitment to ongoing learning and growth. By cultivating strong relationships, adapting to changing circumstances, maintaining a positive outlook, and prioritizing self-care, individuals and organizations can build the resilience they need to thrive in the face of adversity.

What are the threats to developing resilient leadership?

Developing resilient leadership can be challenging, and there are several threats that can hinder the process. Developing resilience requires a willingness to adapt to changing circumstances and to embrace new ways of thinking and doing things. However, individuals and organizations that are resistant to change may struggle to develop the flexibility and adaptability needed to build resilience.

Developing resilience requires a strong support network of family, friends, colleagues, and other members of the community. Nevertheless, individuals and organizations that lack support may struggle to cope with stress and adversity and may be more vulnerable to burnout and other negative outcomes.

Resilience requires a willingness to take calculated risks and to embrace uncertainty. Still, individuals and organizations that are driven by fear and uncertainty may struggle to make decisions and take action, and may be more vulnerable to anxiety, stress, and other negative outcomes.

Resilience requires a commitment to self-care and to maintaining a healthy work-life balance. Regardless of how, individuals and organizations that are chronically overworked and stressed may struggle to maintain the energy, focus, and resilience needed to navigate challenging circumstances.

Developing resilience requires a range of personal and interpersonal skills, as well as access to resources such as time, money, and social support. Yet, individuals and organizations that lack these skills or resources may struggle to develop the resilience they need to thrive in the face of adversity.

Furthermore, developing resilient leadership requires a commitment to ongoing learning and growth, as well as a willingness to embrace change, seek support, and prioritize self-care. By recognizing and addressing potential threats to resilience, individuals and organizations can build the resilience they need to thrive in today's complex and uncertain world.

The big picture reason for developing resilient leadership

The big picture reason for developing resilient leadership is to help individuals and organizations thrive in the face of adversity, uncertainty, and change. In today's fast-paced and rapidly changing world, resilience is a critical skill for leaders in all sectors and industries.

Resilient leadership helps individuals and organizations to navigate complex and uncertain environments, to anticipate and respond to unexpected challenges and opportunities, and to build sustainable organizations that can withstand and recover from crises. It enables leaders to balance short-term needs with long-term goals, to make tough decisions, and to inspire and motivate others to achieve success.

Beyond these practical benefits, resilient leadership also has important social and ethical implications. Leaders who prioritize resilience are able to create organizations that are more adaptive, innovative, and responsive to the needs of their employees, customers, and communities. They are better equipped to tackle complex social and environmental challenges, and to promote social justice, equity, and sustainability.

In short, developing resilient leadership is critical for building a more resilient, sustainable, and equitable world. It enables individuals and organizations to thrive in the face of uncertainty and change, and to create positive social and environmental impacts. By investing in resilient leadership, we can build a better future for ourselves, our organizations, and our communities.

How is resilience really part of a much bigger picture of life?

Resilience is an important aspect of life that is part of a much bigger picture. Life is full of ups and downs, challenges and successes, and resilience is what allows us to navigate these experiences with strength and determination. Building resilience requires developing skills and abilities that allow us to adapt to changing circumstances, overcome adversity, and grow as individuals.

Resilience is part of a much bigger picture because it is essential for achieving long-term success and happiness in life. When we face challenges and setbacks, we have a choice: we can either let these experiences defeat us, or we can use them as opportunities for growth and learning. By developing resilience, we can choose the latter and turn difficult situations into opportunities for personal development and growth.

Resilience is also part of a bigger picture because it allows us to build stronger relationships with others. When we are resilient, we are better able to cope with stress and adversity, which can help us maintain positive relationships with others. We are also better able to support and encourage others who may be going through difficult times, which can help us build stronger, more meaningful connections with others.

Finally, resilience is part of a bigger picture because it allows us to live a more purposeful and meaningful life. When we are resilient, we are better able to pursue our goals and dreams, even in the face of obstacles and challenges. We are also better able to find meaning and purpose in our lives, which can help us achieve a sense of fulfillment and satisfaction.

The Results of Resilient Leadership

Resilient leadership matters because it enables leaders to navigate the challenges and uncertainties of modern work environments and lead effectively in times of crisis. Resilient leaders are better able to manage stress, maintain focus, and make effective decisions in the face of adversity. Leaders who are resilient are better able to manage stress and avoid burnout, which is essential for long-term success as a leader. They are able to maintain their mental and physical health, while also supporting their team members.

Resilient leaders are better able to make effective decisions, even in the face of uncertainty and ambiguity. They are able to approach problems with a clear and focused mind, rather than being overwhelmed by stress or emotion. Resilient leaders can serve as positive role models for their team members, promoting a culture of resilience and adaptability. This can help team members feel more supported and empowered, leading to improved morale and productivity. Resilient leaders are better able to think outside the box and develop creative solutions to problems. They are more likely to see challenges as opportunities for growth and innovation, rather than obstacles to be overcome.

In times of crisis or uncertainty, resilient leaders are better able to manage their own stress and maintain focus, while also supporting their team members. This can help organizations navigate crises more effectively and emerge stronger on the other side. Resilient leadership matters because it enables leaders to navigate the challenges and uncertainties of modern work environments, while also promoting a positive work culture and fostering innovation and creativity. Resilient leaders are better able to manage stress, make effective decisions, and lead effectively in times of crisis, making them essential for the long-term success of any organization.

Key Takeaway

Resilience is part of a much bigger picture of life because it is essential for achieving long-term success and happiness, building stronger relationships with others, and living a purposeful and meaningful life. By developing resilience, we can navigate life's challenges with strength and determination, and turn difficult situations into opportunities for personal growth and development.

Resilient leadership as a grassroots effort

Resilient leadership is often seen as a grassroots effort because it requires individuals and communities to take proactive steps to build resilience and adapt to changing circumstances. Grassroots efforts are often characterized by bottom-up decision-making and community-based problem-solving, which are both important elements of resilient leadership.

Resilient leadership involves fostering a culture of resilience, which can be achieved through education, communication, and collaboration. This requires individuals to take ownership of their own resilience, and to work together with their communities to build resilience at the local level. This bottom-up approach is often more effective than top-down approaches, which can be less responsive to the unique needs and challenges of different communities.

In summary, resilient leadership is a grass roots effort because it requires individuals and communities to take ownership of their own resilience and work together to build a culture of resilience at the local level. By doing so, communities can better adapt to changing circumstances and become more resilient in the face of challenges.

The development of Resilient Leadership is a bottom-up investment

Resilient leadership can be seen as a bottom-up investment because it involves individuals and communities taking proactive steps to build resilience and adapt to changing circumstances. Rather than relying solely on external resources and support, resilient leadership focuses on building local capacity and empowering individuals and communities to take ownership of their own resilience.

Bottom-up investments in resilient leadership can take many forms. For example, individuals can invest in their own resilience by developing skills and habits that promote physical and emotional well-being, such as exercise, meditation, and stress management. Communities can invest in resilient leadership by fostering a culture of collaboration and problem-solving, and by investing in infrastructure and resources that support resilience, such as community centers, emergency preparedness plans, and mental health services.

In contrast to top-down approaches that may rely on external resources and expertise, bottom-up investments in resilient leadership prioritize local knowledge and expertise. This approach can be more effective in building resilience because it is tailored to the unique needs and challenges of each community, and it promotes a sense of ownership and accountability among individuals and groups.

Overall, resilient leadership can be seen as a bottom-up investment because it involves individuals and communities taking ownership of their own resilience and investing in local capacity-building to adapt to changing circumstances. By prioritizing local knowledge and expertise, bottom-up investments in resilient leadership can be more effective in promoting resilience and empowering communities to thrive in the face of challenges.

You will grow in unexpected ways.
Take the journey...Become a Resilient Leader!

Part I Wrap-up and Key Takeaways Summary

The History of Resilient Leadership traces back to the understanding that leaders who possess resilience are better equipped to navigate challenges, setbacks, and uncertainties. Resilience has become a highly valued attribute in the modern world due to its profound impact on leadership effectiveness and organizational success. Resilient leaders possess the ability to adapt, persevere, and bounce back from adversity, which is crucial in today's rapidly changing and unpredictable environments.

Resilience Matters to Leaders because it empowers them to weather storms, inspire their teams, and drive progress even in the face of adversity. Resilient leaders can maintain a positive outlook, make sound decisions under pressure, and effectively manage their emotions and those of their team members. Their ability to stay calm, focused, and adaptable in challenging situations allows them to guide their organizations through turbulent times and foster a culture of resilience.

Resilient Leadership Development occurs at various levels, starting with the individual level. At the individual level, resilience involves developing a growth mindset, cultivating emotional intelligence, and building mental strength to navigate obstacles and setbacks. Leaders must embody resilience themselves before they can effectively lead others through challenging circumstances.

At the leader level, resilience manifests in the ability to inspire and motivate others, provide guidance during uncertain times, and make tough decisions that prioritize long-term goals. Resilient leaders lead by example, creating an environment that fosters growth, learning, and adaptability.

Resilience is also essential at the team development level, where it involves building cohesion, trust, and effective communication among team members. Resilient teams collaborate seamlessly, support one another during difficult periods, and leverage their collective strengths to overcome obstacles.

Furthermore, resilience plays a crucial role at the organizational development level. Resilient organizations have agile structures, robust crisis management strategies, and a culture that embraces change and innovation. They learn from failures, adapt their strategies, and remain proactive in the face of disruptions.

Resilience extends beyond individual organizations and influences cultural and societal development. Resilient cultures promote values such as perseverance, adaptability, and community support. They foster resilience among individuals and organizations, creating a collective capacity to withstand and thrive in the face of challenges.

To develop Resilient Leadership, a Key Model for Expanding Resilient Leadership can be implemented. This model integrates various leadership theories and emphasizes the importance of emotional intelligence as a foundation for resilience. Leaders who possess emotional intelligence can understand and manage their own emotions, navigate interpersonal relationships effectively, and make decisions that consider the well-being of individuals and the organization as a whole.

Developing resilience requires a focus on the key elements of resilience, including self-awareness, self-regulation, empathy, effective communication, and adaptability. By honing these skills and attitudes, leaders can enhance their ability to lead through adversity and uncertainty. However, there are threats to developing resilient leadership, such as resistance to change, fear of failure, and a fixed mindset. Overcoming these threats requires a commitment to continuous learning, embracing discomfort, and fostering a culture that supports resilience.

The big picture reason for developing resilient leadership goes beyond the immediate challenges faced by organizations. Resilient leadership contributes to building a more resilient society as a whole. It creates a ripple effect, inspiring individuals, teams, and organizations to develop their resilience and adaptability, ultimately strengthening the fabric of society.

Resilient leadership is not just about professional success; it is deeply interconnected with personal growth and well-being. The development of resilience extends beyond the workplace and becomes part of a broader life perspective. Resilient leaders are better equipped to navigate the ups and downs of life, maintain balance, and positively impact the lives of those around them.

The development of resilient leadership is not solely a top-down effort; it can be a grass-roots movement. Each individual has the power to cultivate resilience within themselves, and by doing so, they contribute to the collective resilience of their teams, organizations, and society as a whole. Resilient leadership is a bottom-up investment in building a stronger, more adaptable, and thriving future.

Key Takeaways Summary

Leadership Styles

1. While all four leadership styles share some common traits, they differ in their focus, priorities, and characteristics. Transformational leadership emphasizes vision, empowerment, and positive culture, servant leadership prioritizes followers' needs and well-being, authentic leadership emphasizes ethical conduct and transparency, and crisis leadership focuses on managing challenging situations effectively.

2. Each of these leadership styles can contribute to resilience in different ways, by fostering a positive organizational culture, prioritizing the well-

being of followers, promoting transparency and ethical conduct, and effectively managing crises and uncertainty.

3. Emotional intelligence can impact the way in which each leadership style is implemented and the degree to which it contributes to resilience. Leaders with high EI are able to recognize and manage their own emotions, communicate effectively, and respond to the emotions of their followers, all of which are important factors in building resilience.

Developing Resilience

4. Resilience is part of a much bigger picture of life because it is essential for achieving long-term success and happiness, building stronger relationships with others, and living a purposeful and meaningful life. By developing resilience, we can navigate life's challenges with strength and determination, and turn difficult situations into opportunities for personal growth and development.

5. Resilient leadership is a grassroots effort because it requires individuals and communities to take ownership of their own resilience and work together to build a culture of resilience at the local level. By doing so, communities can better adapt to changing circumstances and become more resilient in the face of challenges.

6. Resilient leadership can be seen as a bottom-up investment because it involves individuals and communities taking ownership of their own resilience and investing in local capacity-building to adapt to changing circumstances. By prioritizing local knowledge and expertise, bottom-up investments in resilient leadership can be more effective in promoting resilience and empowering communities to thrive in the face of challenges.

PART II
The Application of Resilient Leadership

Chapter 6
Resilience as a Leadership Model

Resilience as a leadership model can be understood as a framework that emphasizes specific qualities, behaviors, and strategies that leaders can adopt to navigate challenges, overcome adversity, and foster resilience within themselves and their organizations. The resilience model for leadership incorporates a number of elements, which are discussed below.

Self-Awareness: Resilient leaders begin by cultivating self-awareness, understanding their strengths, weaknesses, values, and emotions. They recognize their triggers, stressors, and responses to adversity. This self-awareness enables leaders to effectively manage their own well-being and make informed decisions during challenging times.

Embrace Change: Resilient leaders embrace change and are agile in response to shifting circumstances. They demonstrate flexibility and open-mindedness, allowing them to adjust strategies, plans, and approaches as needed. By being adaptable, leaders can navigate uncertainties, seize opportunities, and guide their organizations towards resilience.

Positive Mindset: Resilient leaders maintain a positive mindset, focusing on possibilities and solutions rather than dwelling on problems. They approach challenges as opportunities for growth and learning, cultivating optimism and a sense of hope. This positive mindset not only influences their own resilience but also inspires and motivates their teams.

Skills Communicators: Resilient leaders are skilled communicators, ensuring clear and timely communication with their teams, stakeholders, and the broader organization. They provide transparent information, set realistic expectations, and keep everyone informed throughout challenging situations. Effective communication fosters trust, reduces uncertainty, and enhances collective resilience.

Build Relationships: Resilient leaders prioritize building strong relationships within their teams and across the organization. They create a supportive work environment that encourages collaboration, trust, and psychological safety. They also establish support systems and encourage peer support, ensuring that individuals can seek help, share concerns, and lean on each other during difficult times.

Make Decisions Under Pressure: Resilient leaders excel at making decisions under pressure. They gather relevant information, consult with experts, consider various perspectives, and make timely and informed choices. They manage risks and uncertainty, recognizing that decisive decision-making is crucial during crises and adversity.

Support a Growth Culture: Resilient leaders foster a culture of continuous learning and growth. They encourage reflection, seek lessons from failures, and celebrate successes. They invest in employee development, provide opportunities for learning, and create a safe space for experimentation and innovation. This focus on learning and growth strengthens the organization's ability to adapt, recover, and thrive in the face of challenges.

Emotional Intelligence: Resilient leaders possess emotional intelligence, understanding and managing their own emotions and those of others. They prioritize well-being and support the well-being of their teams. They promote work-life balance, provide resources for stress management, and create a supportive culture that fosters resilience and psychological well-being.

Resilience as a leadership model involves cultivating self-awareness, adaptability, a positive mindset, effective communication, relationship-building, decision-making under pressure, a learning orientation, emotional intelligence, and well-being. By embodying these qualities and applying these strategies, leaders can foster resilience within themselves and their organizations, guiding them towards success in the face of adversity.

In the next section, we can apply the who, what, when, where, why, and how to different leadership applications in the real world.

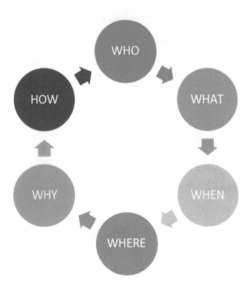

1. THE WHO

Who would want to become a resilient leader?
Anyone who is in a leadership position or aspires to be a leader would benefit from becoming a resilient leader. This includes:

Business executives: Business executives face a wide range of challenges, from economic downturns to disruptive technologies to changing market conditions. Resilience is essential for business leaders who want to navigate these challenges effectively and to maintain their effectiveness over the long term.

Entrepreneurs: Entrepreneurs face many challenges as they launch and grow new ventures, including financial pressures, market uncertainty, and competition. Resilience is essential for entrepreneurs who want to overcome these challenges and to build successful and sustainable businesses.

Nonprofit and healthcare leaders: Nonprofit and healthcare leaders face many challenges, including limited resources, complex regulatory environments, and the need to balance mission and financial sustainability. Resilience is essential for nonprofit leaders who want to navigate these challenges and to achieve their organization's goals.

Government officials: Government officials face many challenges, including budget constraints, political pressure, and the need to serve diverse constituencies. Resilience is essential for government officials who want to navigate these challenges and to deliver effective and efficient services to their communities.

Educational leaders: Educational leaders face many challenges, including budget constraints, changing curriculum standards, and the need to adapt to new technologies. Resilience is essential for educational leaders who want to create a supportive and effective learning environment for their students and staff.

Key Takeaway

Anyone who wants to be an effective leader would benefit from becoming a resilient leader. Resilience is essential for navigating the many challenges that leaders face in today's fast-paced and complex environment.

2. THE WHAT

What is Resilience?

Resilience is the ability to adapt and recover from difficult or stressful situations. In the context of leadership, resilience refers to the ability to navigate challenges and uncertainty while continuing to move forward and achieve goals. Resilient leaders are able to stay focused, motivated, and optimistic even in the face of adversity.

Resilience can be learned or developed as a leader through a combination of experience, mindset, and skill-building. Here are some ways in which leaders can develop resilience:

Mindset: Developing a growth mindset is essential for building resilience as a leader. This means seeing challenges and setbacks as opportunities for learning and growth, rather than as failures. Leaders with a growth mindset are more likely to stay positive and persistent in the face of challenges. Additionally, leaders have a strong "why" for their work and back up plans that may include plan A, B, and C.

Self-Care: Taking care of oneself is crucial for building resilience. Leaders should prioritize their physical and mental health, making time for exercise, rest, and relaxation. By taking care of themselves, leaders are better able to manage stress and stay focused.

Skill-Building: Developing specific skills can help leaders build resilience. For example, developing communication and conflict resolution skills can help leaders navigate challenging situations more effectively. Can improvise, cope, and quickly accept reality to make a plan to move forward. Building problem-solving and decision-making skills can help leaders make effective choices even in uncertain circumstances. They can see the big picture and are systems thinkers.

Learning from Experience: Experience is one of the most important ways in which leaders can develop resilience. Leaders who have faced and overcome challenges in the past are better equipped to handle future challenges. Mindfulness and reflecting on past experiences and identifying lessons learned can help leaders develop a stronger sense of focus while leading to resilience.

Key Takeaway

Resilience is the ability to adapt and recover from difficult or stressful situations. Leaders can develop resilience through a combination of mindset, self-care, skill-building, and learning from experience. By building resilience, leaders are better equipped to navigate challenges and uncertainty, and to continue to achieve their goals despite setbacks.

What factors impact Resilience Development?

Resilience development for leaders is a multifaceted process influenced by a myriad of factors. Beyond the foundational elements previously discussed several other crucial aspects play a pivotal role in shaping a leader's ability to bounce back from adversity.

Social support emerges as a linchpin, with the encouragement and understanding from colleagues, friends, and family proving instrumental in navigating the complexities of leadership. Emotional intelligence, characterized by the adept management of both personal and interpersonal emotions, adds another layer to resilience.

Leaders endowed with a high emotional intelligence quotient are better equipped to weather storms, maintaining composure and optimism amidst trials. Flexibility emerges as a key trait, allowing leaders to adapt to the ever-changing landscape of challenges. Moreover, a profound sense of purpose and meaning in one's professional journey stands as a cornerstone, providing leaders with an enduring motivation that propels them forward in the face of adversity.

As we delve into these additional factors, a comprehensive understanding of resilience development begins to unfold, shedding light on the intricate interplay of various elements that contribute to a leader's capacity to endure and thrive. Here are some additional factors that can impact resilience development:

Social Support: The support of others, such as colleagues, friends, and family, can be an important factor in resilience development. Leaders who have a strong support network are better able to cope with stress and to maintain a positive outlook.

Emotional Intelligence: Emotional intelligence, or the ability to recognize and manage one's own emotions and the emotions of others, can also impact resilience development. Leaders with strong emotional intelligence are better able to manage stress and to maintain a positive mindset in the face of challenges.

Flexibility: Flexibility is another key factor in resilience development. Leaders who are able to adapt to changing circumstances and to approach challenges from different angles are better equipped to maintain their focus and persistence over the long term.

Purpose and Meaning: Having a sense of purpose and meaning in one's work can also impact resilience development. Leaders who are motivated by a sense of purpose and who feel that their work is meaningful are more likely to maintain their focus and persistence, even in the face of significant challenges.

Key Takeaway

There are several other factors that can impact resilience development for leaders, including social support, emotional intelligence, flexibility, and a sense of purpose and meaning. By cultivating these factors, leaders can enhance their ability to adapt and recover from difficult situations, and to maintain a positive outlook even in the face of adversity.

What are the key tools of a resilient leader?

In the demanding landscape of leadership, the tools wielded by resilient leaders serve as the compass and armor guiding them through turbulent waters. These tools form a formidable arsenal, each playing a distinct role in fortifying a leader's capacity to weather challenges and bounce back from setbacks.

At the forefront is self-awareness, a foundational tool that grants resilient leaders an intimate understanding of their internal landscape-strengths, weaknesses, and emotional triggers. Complementing this is emotional intelligence, a dynamic force enabling leaders to navigate the intricate realm of emotions, forging connections with others and fostering a positive environment.

Adaptability emerges as a key instrument, empowering leaders to pivot and recalibrate in response to shifting circumstances. Armed with a positive mindset, resilient leaders cultivate optimism in adversity, viewing challenges as opportunities for growth. Proactive problem-solving becomes a strategic tool, allowing leaders to address issues before they escalate.

The support network, comprising colleagues, mentors, and loved ones, acts as a resilient leader's anchor in times of turbulence. Finally, self-care stands as a non-negotiable tool, ensuring leaders are physically, emotionally, and mentally equipped for the demanding journey.

Together, these tools form a comprehensive toolkit, essential for leaders navigating the complex terrain of leadership with resilience and grace.

The key tools of a resilient leader are as follows:

Self-awareness: A resilient leader is aware of their strengths, weaknesses, and triggers. They are able to recognize their own emotions and reactions to stress, and they have a solid understanding of their own values, goals, and priorities.

Emotional intelligence: A resilient leader has strong emotional intelligence, which allows them to manage their own emotions and to connect with others in a positive and productive way. They are able to empathize with others, build relationships, and resolve conflicts effectively.

Adaptability: A resilient leader is adaptable and flexible, able to adjust their approach and strategies as needed to address changing circumstances or unexpected challenges.

Positive mindset: A resilient leader maintains a positive mindset, even in the face of adversity. They focus on opportunities rather than obstacles, and they are able to maintain a sense of optimism and hope even during difficult times.

Proactive problem-solving: A resilient leader is proactive in addressing problems and challenges, rather than waiting for them to become crises. They are able to identify potential issues early on and take steps to mitigate them before they become more serious.

Support network: A resilient leader has a strong support network of colleagues, mentors, family, and friends. They are able to draw on this network for emotional support, advice, and guidance when needed.

Self-care: A resilient leader takes care of themselves physically, emotionally, and mentally. They prioritize their own well-being, and they engage in activities that promote health, relaxation, and renewal.

Key Takeaway

The key tools of a resilient leader include self-awareness, emotional intelligence, adaptability, positive mindset, proactive problem-solving, support network, and self-care. By developing these tools, leaders can enhance their ability to navigate challenges and maintain their focus and effectiveness over the long term.

What is the survival guide to developing resilience?

Embarking on the journey of developing resilience is akin to crafting a survival guide for navigating the unpredictable terrain of life's challenges. It's a process that demands the honing of skills, attitudes, and behaviors capable of withstanding the storms of difficult and stressful situations.

In this guide to resilience, the importance of forging robust relationships takes center stage; be it with friends, family, or colleagues, these connections serve as vital anchors providing both emotional and practical support. Cultivating a positive mindset emerges as a beacon, illuminating the path through adversity by focusing on gratitude, positive aspects, and the reframing of negative thoughts.

Self-care stands as an indispensable practice, ensuring the resilience-seeker is physically, emotionally, and mentally fortified. Setting realistic goals becomes a strategic compass, offering a sense of accomplishment and self-efficacy. The guide also underscores the significance of honing problem-solving skills, breaking down challenges into manageable steps.

Learning from challenges is a key chapter, emphasizing the transformative power of reflection, feedback, and viewing failures as stepping stones to growth. Finally, seeking support emerges as a crucial chapter, reminding individuals that resilience thrives in the company of those who offer understanding, encouragement, and professional guidance.

In this survival guide to resilience, each strategy forms a chapter, equipping individuals to not only endure life's trials but to emerge stronger and more resilient on the other side. Developing resilience is a process that involves building skills, attitudes, and behaviors that allow individuals to adapt and bounce back from difficult or stressful situations. Here are some strategies that can help individuals develop resilience:

Build strong relationships: Developing and maintaining supportive relationships with friends, family, and colleagues can provide individuals with emotional and practical support during difficult times. These relationships can also help individuals to build a sense of belonging and connection, which is essential for resilience.

Cultivate a positive mindset: Resilient individuals tend to maintain a positive outlook, even in the face of adversity. Cultivating a positive mindset can involve focusing on the things that are going well, practicing gratitude, and reframing negative thoughts.

Practice self-care: Taking care of oneself is essential for building resilience. This can involve getting enough sleep, eating a balanced diet, exercising regularly, and engaging in activities that bring joy and relaxation.

Set realistic goals: Setting achievable goals and taking small steps towards them can help individuals to build a sense of accomplishment and self-efficacy. This can be especially important during times of stress or uncertainty.

Build problem-solving skills: Resilient individuals are often good problem-solvers. Building problem-solving skills can involve breaking problems down into manageable steps, brainstorming solutions, and seeking out information and resources.

Learn from challenges: Resilience involves learning from challenges and using these experiences to grow and develop. This can involve reflecting on past experiences, seeking feedback, and using failures as opportunities for growth.

Seek out support: Asking for help when needed is an important part of resilience. This can involve seeking support from friends, family, or mental health professionals.

Key Takeaway

Developing resilience involves building skills, attitudes, and behaviors that allow individuals to adapt and bounce back from difficult situations. By building strong relationships, cultivating a positive mindset, practicing self-care, setting realistic goals, building problem-solving skills, learning from challenges, and seeking out support, individuals can develop resilience and thrive in the face of adversity.

What is mental fragmentation?

Mental fragmentation refers to a state of psychological disintegration in which an individual experiences a lack of coherence or continuity in their thoughts, feelings, or sense of self. This can manifest in a variety of ways, including dissociation, depersonalization, and emotional numbness.

Mental fragmentation can occur as a result of traumatic experiences such as abuse, neglect, or other forms of violence. It can be a common symptom of conditions like post-traumatic stress disorder (PTSD) and complex trauma and may also be linked to other mental health issues, including anxiety, depression, and borderline personality disorder.

Symptoms of mental fragmentation can include:

• feelings of detachment or disconnection from oneself or others
• loss of a sense of identity or self
• distorted perceptions of reality
• inability to regulate emotions
• memory problems or gaps in memory
• difficulty with concentration and attention
• intrusive thoughts or flashbacks

Treatment for mental fragmentation typically involves a combination of therapy and medication, depending on the underlying causes and symptoms. Therapy may focus on helping individuals process traumatic experiences and develop coping strategies to manage symptoms. Medications such as antidepressants or anti-anxiety medications may also be prescribed to address specific symptoms such as depression, anxiety, or insomnia.

Key Takeaway

Mental fragmentation is a complex and challenging experience that can have significant impacts on an individual's mental and emotional well-being. With appropriate treatment and support, it may be possible to recover a sense of coherence and continuity in one's thoughts, feelings, and sense of self, promoting healing and recovery from trauma.

What relates mental fragmentation to resilience?

Mental fragmentation can have a negative impact on an individual's resilience, as it can make it more difficult to cope with stress and adversity. When an individual experiences mental fragmentation, their thoughts, feelings, and sense of self may become disjointed, making it harder to process and adapt to challenging situations.

In order to be resilient, individuals need to be able to effectively cope with stress and adversity and bounce back from setbacks. However, mental fragmentation can interfere with this process by making it more difficult to regulate emotions, focus attention, and maintain a sense of self-efficacy.

That being said, it is important to note that resilience is a complex construct that can manifest in different ways for different individuals. While mental fragmentation may make it more difficult to be resilient, it is not necessarily a barrier to resilience. With appropriate treatment and support, individuals who have experienced mental fragmentation may be able to develop the skills and strategies necessary to cope with stress and adversity and cultivate a sense of resilience.

Therapeutic interventions can be particularly helpful in promoting resilience for individuals who have experienced mental fragmentation. These therapies are designed to help individuals process traumatic experiences, regulate emotions, and develop coping skills that can enhance resilience and improve overall well-being. By addressing the underlying causes of mental fragmentation and providing support for recovery, it may be possible to cultivate resilience and promote healing and growth.

3. THE WHEN

When are resilient leaders needed in teams or organizations?

Resilient leaders are needed in teams or organizations when facing challenges or uncertain situations that may have a significant impact on the team or organization. Some examples of when resilient leaders are needed include:

During times of crisis: Resilient leaders are essential during times of crisis, such as natural disasters, economic downturns, or pandemics. They are able to remain calm and focused, communicate effectively with their team, and adapt to changing circumstances to lead their team through the crisis.

During times of change: Resilient leaders are also needed during times of change, such as mergers, acquisitions, or restructuring. They are able to navigate the uncertainties and challenges of change, provide stability and direction to their team, and help the team adapt to the new reality.

During periods of rapid growth: Resilient leaders are essential during periods of rapid growth, as they are able to manage the challenges of scaling up operations, hiring new employees, and managing increased complexity. They are able to maintain a clear vision and strategy, communicate effectively with their team, and adapt to changing circumstances to ensure the growth is sustainable.

When dealing with difficult or complex projects: Resilient leaders are also needed when dealing with difficult or complex projects, such as research and development or implementing new technologies. They are able to manage the risks and uncertainties of these projects, provide direction and support to their team, and adapt to changing circumstances to ensure the project's success.

Key Takeaway

Resilient leaders are needed in teams or organizations when facing challenges, uncertainties, or changes that require strong leadership to navigate. They are able to provide stability, direction, and support to their team, and adapt to changing circumstances to ensure the success of the team or organization.

When does a leader become a resilient leader?

A leader becomes a resilient leader when they are able to effectively cope with stress and overcome challenges. Resilient leaders are able to adapt to changes, maintain a positive mindset, and lead their teams through difficult times. They have the ability to bounce back from setbacks, remain focused on their goals, and inspire others to do the same.

Becoming a resilient leader is not a one-time event, but rather a process that takes time and intentional effort. It requires a commitment to personal growth and development, as well as a willingness to learn from past experiences and embrace new challenges.

Leaders can become more resilient by developing skills such as emotional intelligence, adaptability, grit, and self-awareness. They can also cultivate resilience by building a support system, practicing self-care, setting realistic goals, learning from past experiences, and developing a positive mindset.

Key Takeaway
A leader becomes a resilient leader when they are able to navigate difficult situations with grace and composure, while inspiring their teams to do the same. Developing resilience takes time and effort and the journey is not a one fits all path.

4. THE WHERE

Where are resilient leaders most needed?
In the dynamic tapestry of industries, resilient leaders emerge as indispensable catalysts for success, providing steadiness in the face of uncertainty. While the need for resilience is pervasive across all sectors, certain industries demand leaders with an exceptional capacity to navigate tumultuous terrains.

In healthcare, where professionals grapple with demanding schedules, high stress, and rapid decision-making, resilient leaders are essential to ensuring the well-being of both their teams and patients. The technology sector, marked by constant evolution and disruption, requires leaders capable of managing uncertainties and steering teams with strategic precision.

Resilient leaders in finance navigate the intricate landscape of market volatility and economic uncertainty, providing stability and adaptability to ensure the success of their companies and clients. In education, an industry characterized by perpetual change, resilient leaders play a pivotal role in managing challenges, guiding teams, and adapting to evolving circumstances to deliver the best possible education.

Nonprofit organizations, facing unique challenges such as limited resources and complex regulatory environments, rely on resilient leaders to navigate these complexities and steer their organizations towards achieving their mission-driven goals. In these industries and beyond, the presence of resilient leaders is not just beneficial-it is integral to overcoming challenges, fostering growth, and ensuring sustained success. Resilient leaders are needed in every industry, but there are some industries where resilience is particularly important. These include:

Healthcare: Healthcare professionals face significant challenges, including long hours, high stress, and the need to make critical decisions quickly. Resilient leaders in healthcare are able to navigate these challenges, provide support to their teams, and adapt to changing circumstances to ensure the safety and well-being of their patients.

Technology: The technology industry is constantly evolving, with new innovations and disruptions happening regularly. Resilient leaders in technology are able to manage the uncertainties and complexities of the industry, provide strategic direction to their teams, and adapt to changing circumstances to ensure their companies remain competitive.

Finance: The finance industry is subject to significant market volatility and economic uncertainty. Resilient leaders in finance are able to navigate these challenges, provide stability and direction to their teams, and adapt to changing circumstances to ensure the success of their companies and clients.

Education: The education industry is constantly evolving, with new technologies and curriculum standards emerging regularly. Resilient leaders in education are able to manage the challenges of change, provide support and direction to their teams, and adapt to changing circumstances to ensure their students receive the best education possible.

Nonprofit: Nonprofit organizations face unique challenges, including limited resources, complex regulatory environments, and the need to balance mission and financial sustainability. Resilient leaders in nonprofits are able to navigate these challenges, provide strategic direction to their teams, and adapt to changing circumstances to ensure their organizations achieve their goals.

Key Takeaway

Resilient leaders are needed in every industry, but particularly in industries where the challenges are significant and the need for adaptability and agility is high. Resilient leaders play a critical role across diverse industries, offering stability in the face of uncertainty and guiding teams through challenges.

In healthcare, where high stress and rapid decision-making are constants, resilient leaders ensure the well-being of both teams and patients. The technology sector demands leaders capable of navigating constant evolution, while resilient leaders in finance manage market volatility and economic uncertainty.

In education, marked by perpetual change, resilient leaders adapt to evolving circumstances for the benefit of students. Nonprofit organizations, facing unique challenges, rely on resilient leaders to navigate complexities and steer toward mission-driven goals. While resilience is universally valuable, it proves particularly crucial in industries where unpredictability is inherent, ensuring sustained success and fostering growth.

Where are resilient leaders NOT needed?

In the intricate fabric of leadership, the value of resilient leaders extends far and wide, offering a compass through turbulent waters and inspiring teams to weather storms. While their efficacy is undeniable in navigating uncertainty, there may be perceptions that in exceptionally stable and predictable environments, the need for resilience is diminished.

In such settings, leaders emphasizing stability and consistency may seem more fitting. However, the unexpected can still unfurl even in the most stable of environments, and it is in these unforeseen challenges that the true worth of a resilient leader becomes apparent.

Even when change is minimal, the potential for growth and improvement persists, and a resilient leader serves as a guide, steering their team toward success and continuous development. Thus, the value of resilience transcends the ebb and flow of stability, offering not just a response to challenges but a proactive force for growth and triumph in any leadership landscape.

Resilient leaders can be valuable in almost any setting, as they are able to effectively navigate difficult situations and inspire their teams to do the same. However, it is possible that in some very stable or predictable environments where there is little change or uncertainty, resilient leaders may not be as necessary. In these cases, leaders who focus more on maintaining stability and consistency may be more appropriate.

That being said, even in stable environments, unexpected challenges can arise, and having a leader with resilience and adaptability can be valuable in these situations. Additionally, even in predictable environments, there may still be opportunities for growth and improvement, and a resilient leader can help guide their team towards success and continued development.

Key Takeaway

While resilient leaders may be more necessary in certain settings, their skills and abilities can be valuable in almost any situation. In the vast landscape of leadership, resilient leaders find their value in navigating uncertainty and inspiring teams through challenges.

While stability and predictability may suggest diminished necessity for resilience, the unforeseen can still surface even in the most stable environments. In such instances, the worth of resilient leaders becomes evident as they guide teams through unexpected challenges.

Even in seemingly predictable settings, the potential for growth persists, and resilient leaders serve as proactive guides, steering teams toward success and continuous development. The recognition of resilience as a force for growth and triumph underscores its universal applicability, demonstrating that in any leadership landscape, resilience remains an invaluable quality, capable of navigating both calm waters and turbulent seas.

5. THE WHY

Why is resilience important to those in leadership roles?
In the realm of leadership, resilience stands as a cornerstone for success, offering a multifaceted toolkit to navigate the complexities inherent in leadership roles. Leaders grapple with a spectrum of challenges, from managing personnel dynamics to steering through intricate business landscapes. Resilience becomes a vital asset, empowering leaders to remain focused, motivated, and adaptive in the face of these challenges.

Beyond the operational intricacies, leadership roles often come with a significant dose of stress. The ability to manage stress is not just a matter of personal well-being but is intrinsic to sustaining productivity. Resilience equips leaders with the tools to not only cope with stress but to maintain a positive mindset even when adversity looms large.

Beyond personal attributes, the influence of resilient leaders extends to the interpersonal realm. They are perceived as reliable and trustworthy, navigating challenges with consistency over time, thereby building trust among employees, stakeholders, and key collaborators. Additionally, resilient leaders serve as beacons, modeling behaviors that inspire resilience in others.

By embracing a proactive and adaptable approach to challenges, they contribute to fostering a resilient culture within their organizations. Furthermore, as leaders set their sights on long-term goals, resilience becomes an indispensable ally, providing the endurance and commitment needed to overcome obstacles and stay true to their vision.

In essence, resilience is not just a personal attribute for leaders; it is a transformative force that shapes their journey and influences the cultures they cultivate within their organizations.

Resilience is important to those in leadership roles for several reasons:

Dealing with challenges: Leaders face a variety of challenges in their roles, from managing difficult employees to navigating complex business environments. Resilience helps leaders to stay focused, motivated, and adaptive in the face of these challenges.

Coping with stress: Leadership roles can be stressful, and the ability to manage stress is essential for maintaining productivity and well-being. Resilience helps leaders to cope with stress and to maintain a positive mindset, even in the face of adversity.

Building trust: Resilient leaders are seen as reliable and trustworthy, as they are able to navigate challenges and maintain a consistent approach over time. This can help to build trust and confidence among employees, stakeholders, and other key stakeholders.

Modeling behavior: Leaders who demonstrate resilience are more likely to inspire resilience in others. By modeling a proactive and adaptable approach to challenges, leaders can help to create a culture of resilience within their organizations.

Achieving goals: Resilience is essential for achieving long-term goals, as it helps leaders to maintain their focus and persistence over time. Leaders who are resilient are better equipped to overcome obstacles and to stay committed to their vision and goals, even in the face of setbacks.

Key Takeaway

Resilience is important to those in leadership roles because it helps them to deal with challenges, cope with stress, build trust, model behavior, and achieve goals. By developing resilience, leaders can enhance their ability to lead effectively and to achieve long-term success for themselves and their organizations.

6. THE HOW

How is grit part of resilience development?

Grit is a key component of resilience development, as it refers to the ability to persevere in the face of adversity and to maintain a long-term goal despite setbacks. Gritty individuals are able to remain focused and persistent, even when faced with challenges or obstacles.

Grit can be developed through a combination of experience, mindset, and skill-building. Here are some ways in which leaders can develop grit as part of resilience development:

Mindset: Developing a growth mindset is essential for building grit. This means seeing challenges as opportunities for learning and growth, rather than as obstacles. Leaders with a growth mindset are more likely to stay focused and persistent in the face of setbacks.

Perseverance: Perseverance is a key element of grit, as it involves the ability to continue working towards a goal, even when progress is slow or difficult. Leaders can develop perseverance by setting small, achievable goals and focusing on the progress made towards those goals.

Resilience: Developing resilience is closely linked to developing grit. Leaders who are able to adapt and recover from difficult situations are better equipped to maintain their focus and persistence over the long term.

Learning from Experience: Experience is one of the most important ways in which leaders can develop grit. Leaders who have faced and overcome challenges in the past are better equipped to maintain their focus and persistence in the face of future challenges.

Key Takeaway

Grit is a key component of resilience development, as it involves the ability to persevere in the face of adversity and to maintain a long-term goal despite setbacks. Leaders can develop grit by developing a growth mindset, building perseverance, developing resilience, and learning from experience. By building grit, leaders are better equipped to maintain their focus and persistence, they keep going, even in the face of significant challenges.

Are grit and mental toughness the same thing?

Mental toughness refers to the ability to remain focused, confident, and resilient in the face of adversity, stress, or pressure. It involves maintaining a strong sense of self-belief, staying calm under pressure, and persevering through difficult situations. Mental toughness is often associated with high-performance athletes and military personnel, but it can also be an important trait for leaders.

Grit, on the other hand, is the ability to maintain a long-term goal despite setbacks, and to persevere in the face of adversity. Grit involves persistence, resilience, and a passion for achieving one's goals. While mental toughness can be an important factor in developing grit, it also involves the ability to maintain a long-term focus and to remain committed to one's goals over time.

Is mental toughness the same as resilience?

Mental toughness and resilience are related concepts but not exactly the same. While they share some similarities, they also have distinct characteristics.

Resilience refers to the ability to bounce back, recover, and adapt in the face of adversity, challenges, or setbacks. It involves the capacity to withstand stress, maintain well-being, and effectively navigate difficult situations. Resilience encompasses emotional, cognitive, and behavioral aspects and involves the ability to cope with and recover from adversity.

Mental toughness, on the other hand, refers to the mindset, attitudes, and psychological traits that enable individuals to persevere and perform at their best, particularly in high-pressure or demanding situations. It involves the ability to stay focused, motivated, and resilient in the face of obstacles, setbacks, or intense competition.

Here are some key distinctions between resilience and mental toughness:

Scope: Resilience is a broader concept that encompasses various aspects of well-being, adaptability, and coping with adversity. It encompasses emotional, cognitive, and behavioral resilience. Mental toughness, on the other hand, specifically focuses on psychological traits and attitudes related to performance and persistence in challenging situations.

Response to adversity: Resilience emphasizes the ability to bounce back, recover, and adapt after facing adversity. It includes emotional and psychological well-being throughout the process. Mental toughness, on the other hand, emphasizes the ability to maintain focus, motivation, and performance in the face of adversity. It relates more specifically to an individual's mindset and approach to challenges.

Context: Resilience is applicable across various domains of life, including personal, professional, and social aspects. It is relevant to both everyday stressors and significant life events. Mental toughness, while also applicable to various areas, is often associated with competitive environments, such as sports, high-pressure work settings, or challenging performance scenarios.

Components: Resilience involves multiple components, including emotional regulation, problem-solving skills, social support, and adaptive coping strategies. Mental toughness, on the other hand, emphasizes psychological attributes such as confidence, perseverance, determination, focus, and optimism.

While mental toughness can contribute to resilience, resilience is a broader construct that encompasses various factors beyond mental toughness. Resilience includes emotional and cognitive aspects, coping strategies, social support, and adaptive behaviors. Mental toughness, on the other hand, focuses more narrowly on the psychological traits and attitudes that contribute to persistence and performance in challenging situations.

Key Takeaway

While mental toughness and grit share some similarities, they are not the same thing. Both mental toughness and grit can be important traits for leaders. Developing both can help leaders to maintain their focus, persistence, and resilience in the face of challenges and setbacks.

Chapter 7
The Mind, Emotions, and Resilience

The detailed exploration of various aspects related to resilience in this chapter provides a comprehensive understanding of its applications and impact. The analogies drawn between resilience and different scenarios, such as psychological trauma, uncertainty, hope, hardships, and the establishment of a new normal, offer a rich perspective on the versatility of resilience.

The narratives provided explain how resilience is not only crucial in times of crisis but also an integral part of personal growth, well-being, and overcoming various life challenges. The inclusion of spiritual convictions, the role of structure and routine, and the comparison with nature adds depth to the discussion, highlighting the multifaceted nature of resilience.

The exploration of loneliness and its connection to resilience demonstrates the social aspect of this quality, emphasizing the importance of building connections and seeking support. The insights into how suffering can contribute to resilience by fostering coping skills and personal growth provide a nuanced perspective on the relationship between adversity and strength.

Overall, the exploration effectively communicates the significance of resilience in diverse aspects of life, showcasing its transformative power in navigating the complexities of the human experience.

How does resilience apply to psychological trauma?

Resilience is an important factor in helping individuals recover from psychological trauma. Psychological trauma refers to experiences that are emotionally and psychologically overwhelming and can cause long-lasting effects on an individual's mental health and well-being. Trauma can result from a variety of events, including natural disasters, interpersonal violence, and accidents.

Resilience can help individuals to recover from trauma by allowing them to adapt to the challenges and changes that arise in the aftermath of the traumatic event. Resilience can help individuals to build the skills and strategies necessary to cope with their emotions, manage their thoughts, and work towards recovery. Resilient individuals are better able to find meaning and purpose in their experiences and develop a sense of hope for the future.

Resilience can also help individuals to maintain healthy relationships and social support systems, which are critical for recovery from trauma. Resilient individuals are more likely to seek out support from friends, family, and mental health professionals, which can help them to process their emotions and work towards healing.

It's important to note that building resilience after trauma is a process that takes time and effort. It can involve therapy, self-care, and the development of new coping strategies. It's important for individuals to seek professional help when needed and to recognize that healing is a journey, not a destination.

Key Takeaway

Resilience plays a crucial role in helping individuals recover from psychological trauma. It allows individuals to adapt to the challenges of trauma and develop the skills and strategies necessary to cope, recover, and move forward in their lives.

How does resilience impact states of uncertainty?

Resilience can have a significant impact on an individual's ability to cope with states of uncertainty. Uncertainty refers to situations where the outcome is unknown or unpredictable, which can create feelings of anxiety, stress, and fear.

Resilience can help individuals to manage these feelings and develop effective coping strategies. Resilient individuals are better able to regulate their emotions and thoughts, which can help them to stay calm and focused during uncertain times. They are also more likely to be flexible and adaptable in the face of change, which can be especially important during times of uncertainty when circumstances are constantly evolving.

Resilient individuals are also more likely to seek out information and support, which can help them to navigate uncertainty more effectively. They are more likely to engage in problem-solving behaviors, which can help them to find solutions to the challenges they are facing.

Moreover, resilient individuals often have a sense of purpose and meaning in their lives, which can provide a sense of stability and direction during uncertain times. They may also have a strong support system that can provide emotional and practical support during challenging times.

Key Takeaway

Resilience can help individuals to cope with states of uncertainty by allowing them to regulate their emotions and thoughts, remain adaptable and flexible, seek out information and support, engage in problem-solving behaviors, and find meaning and purpose in their lives.

How is hope part of resilience?

Hope is an essential component of resilience. Resilience is the ability to adapt and bounce back from difficult or stressful situations, and hope is the belief that things will get better in the future. Having hope can help individuals to maintain a positive outlook, even in the face of adversity.

Hope can provide individuals with a sense of purpose and direction, which can be especially important during challenging times. It can motivate individuals to set goals and work towards positive outcomes, even when faced with obstacles or setbacks. This sense of purpose and direction can help individuals to maintain their resilience and bounce back from difficult situations.

Moreover, hope can provide individuals with a sense of agency and control over their lives. It can help individuals to believe that they have the power to create positive change and overcome challenges. This sense of agency and control can be especially important during times when individuals may feel powerless or out of control.

Finally, hope can provide individuals with a sense of connection and support. It can help individuals to maintain relationships and social connections, which are critical for resilience. Having hope can also help individuals to seek out support and resources when needed, which can help them to overcome challenges and build resilience.

Key Takeaway

Hope is an essential part of resilience. It provides individuals with a sense of purpose and direction, a sense of agency and control, and a sense of connection and support. By cultivating hope, individuals can build their resilience and bounce back from difficult situations.

How does resilience help one overcome hardship?

Resilience helps individuals to overcome hardships by providing them with the ability to adapt and bounce back from difficult or stressful situations. When faced with a hardship, resilient individuals are better able to regulate their emotions and thoughts, which allows them to maintain a sense of perspective and cope effectively with the situation.

Resilient individuals are also more likely to seek out support and resources when needed. They may turn to friends, family, or mental health professionals for help, which can provide them with emotional and practical support. This support can help individuals to feel less alone and more capable of overcoming their hardships.

Moreover, resilient individuals are often able to find meaning and purpose in their experiences. They may use their hardship as an opportunity to learn and grow, to develop new skills, or to deepen their relationships. This sense of purpose and meaning can provide individuals with a sense of direction and motivation, even during challenging times.

Finally, resilient individuals are often able to maintain a positive outlook, even in the face of adversity. They may focus on the things that they can control and take small steps towards positive change. This positive outlook can help individuals to maintain their resilience and bounce back from difficult situations.

Key Takeaway

Resilience helps individuals to overcome hardships by allowing them to regulate their emotions and thoughts, seek out support and resources, find meaning and purpose in their experiences, and maintain a positive outlook. By building resilience, individuals can become better equipped to overcome the challenges that life throws their way.

How does resilience help establish a new normal?

Resilience can help individuals establish a new normal by allowing them to adapt and adjust to changes in their lives. When faced with a significant change or challenge, individuals may need to create a new normal or routine that accommodates their new circumstances. Resilience can help individuals to do this in a way that allows them to maintain their well-being and move forward in a positive direction.

Resilient individuals are better able to regulate their emotions and thoughts, which can help them to approach the process of establishing a new normal with a clear and focused mindset. They are also more likely to be flexible and adaptable in the face of change, which can help them to adjust their routines and behaviors in response to new circumstances.

Moreover, resilient individuals are often able to find meaning and purpose in their experiences. This can be especially important during times of transition, when individuals may be struggling to make sense of their new circumstances. By finding meaning and purpose, individuals can create a sense of continuity and stability, even in the midst of change.

Finally, resilient individuals are often able to maintain a positive outlook, even in the face of adversity. This positive outlook can help individuals to approach the process of establishing a new normal with a sense of hope and optimism, which can be essential for maintaining motivation and moving forward.

Key Takeaway

Resilience can help individuals establish a new normal by allowing them to regulate their emotions and thoughts, be flexible and adaptable, find meaning and purpose, and maintain a positive outlook. By building resilience, individuals can adapt to change and create a new normal that allows them to thrive.

How does resilience negate fear?

Resilience and fear are two different concepts that can coexist but are not necessarily directly related to each other. However, resilience can help to mitigate the impact of fear and reduce its negative effects.

Resilience refers to the ability to bounce back and recover from adversity or stress. It involves developing coping strategies, adapting to change, and maintaining a positive outlook in the face of challenges. By cultivating resilience, individuals can build their capacity to handle difficult situations, which can reduce the intensity and duration of fear and anxiety.

Fear, on the other hand, is an emotional response to perceived danger or threat. It can be a natural and adaptive response that helps individuals to protect themselves from harm. However, excessive or prolonged fear can have negative effects on mental and physical health, relationships, and quality of life.

When individuals develop resilience, they become better equipped to handle the challenges that trigger fear. They may be more likely to take proactive steps to address the situation, seek support from others, and maintain a sense of control over their lives. This can reduce the intensity and duration of fear and help individuals to recover more quickly from stressful situations.

Key Takeaway

Resilience does not negate fear, but it can help individuals to manage and cope with fear more effectively, which can reduce its negative impact on their lives.

How are resilience and nourishing the soul related?

Resilience and nourishing the soul are related in that they both involve building and maintaining a sense of inner strength and well-being.

Resilience refers to the ability to adapt and recover from difficult situations, which can involve physical, mental, and emotional challenges. Developing resilience requires building coping skills, maintaining positive relationships, and cultivating a sense of purpose and meaning in life. Nourishing the soul, on the other hand, involves activities that promote a sense of spiritual well-being and connection to a higher power or sense of purpose. This can include practices such as prayer, meditation, spending time in nature, engaging in creative activities, or participating in community service.

Both resilience and nourishing the soul involve developing a sense of inner strength and resilience that can help individuals to cope with adversity and maintain a sense of well-being, even in challenging circumstances. By engaging in activities that promote resilience and spiritual well-being, individuals can build their capacity to handle stress, find meaning and purpose in their lives, and maintain a positive outlook, which can contribute to overall health and well-being.

How does the act of suffering help to develop resilience?

Suffering can be a difficult and painful experience, but it can also help to develop resilience by providing an opportunity for individuals to build their capacity to cope with adversity.

When individuals experience suffering, they may be forced to confront their own vulnerabilities and limitations and may feel overwhelmed by the challenges they face. However, through the process of coping with suffering, individuals can develop a range of skills and resources that can help them to become more resilient in the face of future challenges.

Some ways that suffering can help to develop resilience include:

Building coping skills: When individuals experience suffering, they may be forced to develop new coping strategies to manage their emotions, thoughts, and behaviors. Through trial and error, they can learn which strategies work best for them, and can develop a repertoire of skills that can be applied to future challenges.

Developing perspective: Suffering can also provide individuals with a new perspective on life and can help them to prioritize what is truly important to them. This can help them to find greater meaning and purpose in their lives, which can be a source of strength in times of difficulty.

Enhancing social support: Suffering can also bring individuals closer to others who may be going through similar experiences. This can provide a sense of community and social support, which can be a source of comfort and strength in times of hardship.

Fostering personal growth: Through the process of coping with suffering, individuals can develop a greater sense of self-awareness, and may become more resilient and adaptable as a result. They may also become more compassionate and empathetic towards others who are going through difficult times.

Key Takeaway

While suffering can be a challenging and painful experience, it can also provide an opportunity for individuals to develop resilience and other important life skills. By learning to cope with adversity, individuals can become more capable of managing future challenges, and can cultivate a greater sense of well-being and purpose in their lives.

How can the reserves of resilience sustain an individual?

Reserves of resilience refer to the internal and external resources that individuals can draw upon to cope with adversity and recover from stress or trauma. These resources can help individuals to maintain a sense of well-being, even in the face of difficult circumstances. Reserves of resilience can include:

Personal strengths: Personal strength includes qualities such as optimism, self-efficacy, and a sense of purpose or meaning in life. These qualities can provide a sense of internal strength and motivation and can help individuals to maintain a positive outlook even in difficult times.

Social support: Social support encompasses the presence of supportive relationships, such as family, friends, and community members. Social support can provide emotional comfort, practical assistance, and a sense of belonging, which can all contribute to resilience.

Coping strategies: Coping strategies have a range of adaptive coping strategies such as problem-solving, emotion regulation, and mindfulness. These strategies can help individuals to manage their thoughts and emotions, and to navigate difficult situations more effectively.

Physical health: Maintaining physical health requires activity and choices that support physical health such as exercise, healthy eating, and adequate sleep. Physical health can contribute to mental and emotional well-being, and can help individuals to better manage stress.

Spiritual or religious beliefs: Spirituality includes a sense of connection to a higher power, a belief in a greater purpose or meaning, or engagement in spiritual practices such as prayer or meditation. These beliefs and practices can provide a sense of inner strength and resilience, and can help individuals to find meaning and purpose in difficult times.

Key Takeaway

By cultivating and maintaining these reserves of resilience, individuals can build their capacity to cope with adversity and recover from stress or trauma. This can help to promote overall well-being and can contribute to a sense of inner strength and resilience that can support individuals throughout their lives. Resilience has reserves and can sustain an individual for a long time but when the reserves are exhausted the individual will desire or require a change.

How does trauma build on more trauma?

Trauma can build on more trauma through a process known as the "trauma cascade" or "trauma chain reaction." This refers to the idea that experiencing one traumatic event can increase an individual's vulnerability to experiencing additional traumas in the future, creating a cycle of trauma and adversity.

There are several reasons why trauma can build on more trauma including:

Psychological impact: Traumatic events can have a profound impact on an individual's mental health and well-being, leading to symptoms such as anxiety, depression, and post-traumatic stress disorder (PTSD). These symptoms can impair an individual's ability to cope with future stressors, making them more vulnerable to experiencing additional traumas.

Behavioral patterns: Trauma can also lead to the development of maladaptive coping strategies, such as substance abuse, self-harm, or risky behaviors. These behaviors can increase an individual's risk of experiencing additional traumas or adverse events.

Social factors: Trauma can also affect an individual's social and interpersonal relationships, leading to isolation, distrust, and difficulty forming close connections with others. This can increase an individual's vulnerability to experiencing additional traumas, as they may lack the social support or protective factors necessary to cope with adversity.

Environmental factors: Trauma can also be linked to environmental factors such as poverty, discrimination, and violence. These factors can create a cycle of adversity that increases an individual's risk of experiencing additional traumas.

Key Takeaway

Trauma can build on more trauma through a complex interplay of psychological, behavioral, social, and environmental factors. By understanding the trauma cascade and the ways in which trauma can impact an individual's life, it may be possible to develop more effective interventions and supports to break the cycle of trauma and promote healing and resilience.

How is resilience related to well-being?

Resilience is closely related to well-being, as it can help individuals to cope with adversity and maintain a sense of physical, emotional, and psychological health even in the face of difficult circumstances. Resilience can contribute to well-being in several ways:

Improved mental health: Resilience can help individuals to cope with stress and trauma, reducing the risk of developing mental health problems such as anxiety, depression, and post-traumatic stress disorder (PTSD). By promoting a more positive outlook and enhancing coping skills, resilience can support overall mental health and well-being.

Enhanced physical health: Resilience can also support physical health by reducing stress levels and promoting healthy lifestyle habits such as exercise and good nutrition. This can help to reduce the risk of developing chronic health problems such as cardiovascular disease and diabetes, and can support overall physical well-being.

Greater life satisfaction: Resilience can contribute to a greater sense of life satisfaction and happiness, as individuals who are more resilient may be better able to manage stress and adapt to changing circumstances. This can help to promote a sense of purpose and meaning in life, contributing to overall well-being.

Improved social connections: Resilience can also support social connections, as individuals who are more resilient may be better able to maintain supportive relationships and seek out help when needed. This can provide a sense of belonging and connection to others, which can contribute to overall well-being.

Key Takeaway

Resilience is closely related to well-being, as it can support mental and physical health, enhance life satisfaction, and promote social connections. By developing and maintaining resilience, individuals can cultivate a greater sense of well-being and resilience in the face of adversity.

How does structure and routine help build resilience?

Structure can play an important role in building resilience because it provides a framework for organizing and managing our lives. When we have structure in our daily routines and activities, we are better able to cope with stress and adversity. Here are some ways that structure can help build resilience:

Provides a sense of predictability: Having a structured routine can help us feel more in control of our lives and give us a sense of predictability. This can be especially helpful during times of uncertainty or change.

Creates a sense of purpose: When we have a structure to our day, we are more likely to have a sense of purpose and direction. This can help us stay motivated and focused on our goals, even in the face of challenges.

Builds good habits: Structure can help us develop good habits, such as regular exercise, healthy eating, and consistent sleep patterns. These habits can contribute to our overall physical and mental well-being, making us better able to handle stress and adversity.

Provides a support system: Structure can help us establish a support system of family, friends, and other resources that can help us cope with difficult situations. This can be especially important during times of crisis or trauma.

Key Takeaway

Having structure in our lives can help us build resilience by providing a sense of predictability, purpose, good habits, and support. By developing these skills, we can better manage stress and adversity and bounce back from difficult situations.

How does building resilience equal unparalleled times of self-growth?

Building resilience involves developing the capacity to adapt and bounce back from adversity and challenges. This process often requires us to step out of our comfort zones and face difficult situations that can be uncomfortable or even painful. However, by embracing these challenges and working through them, we can experience unparalleled times of self-growth and personal development.

One way that building resilience can lead to self-growth is by helping us develop a growth mindset. A growth mindset is the belief that our abilities and intelligence can be developed through effort and learning. When we face challenges, we can either view them as opportunities for growth or as threats to our sense of self. By embracing challenges and viewing them as opportunities to learn and grow, we can develop a growth mindset that allows us to approach new situations with confidence and resilience.

Another way that building resilience can lead to self-growth is by helping us develop greater self-awareness. When we face difficult situations, we are forced to confront our own limitations, fears, and insecurities. By recognizing and acknowledging these aspects of ourselves, we can develop greater self-awareness and self-acceptance. This, in turn, can help us build stronger relationships with others and cultivate a greater sense of purpose and meaning in our lives.

How do spiritual convictions ground resilience?

Spiritual convictions can provide a grounding force that helps people build resilience in the face of adversity. Whether it is through religious beliefs, personal values, or a sense of connection to a higher power, spiritual convictions can provide a source of meaning and purpose that can help people navigate difficult times.

One way that spiritual convictions can ground resilience is by providing a sense of perspective. When we face challenges, it can be easy to get caught up in the immediate difficulties and lose sight of the bigger picture. Spiritual convictions can help us see our struggles in the context of a larger purpose or plan, which can give us the strength and determination to keep moving forward.

Spiritual convictions can also provide a source of comfort and solace during difficult times. Whether through prayer, meditation, or other spiritual practices, people can find a sense of peace and calm in the midst of chaos and uncertainty. This can help them cope with stress and anxiety, and give them the strength to persevere through difficult times.

Finally, spiritual convictions can provide a sense of community and support that can help people build resilience. Many religious and spiritual traditions emphasize the importance of caring for others and supporting those in need. By connecting with others who share our spiritual beliefs, we can find a sense of belonging and support that can help us navigate difficult times.

Key Takeaway

Spiritual convictions can ground resilience by providing a sense of perspective, comfort, and community. By connecting with a larger purpose or plan, finding solace in spiritual practices, and connecting with others who share our beliefs, we can find the strength and determination to persevere through difficult times.

How is loneliness curbed with resilience?

Loneliness can be a challenging experience, but resilience can play a key role in helping individuals overcome feelings of isolation and loneliness. Resilience involves developing skills and abilities that allow us to cope with stress and adversity, and this can be particularly important when it comes to dealing with feelings of loneliness.

One way that resilience can help curb loneliness is by fostering a sense of self-efficacy. When we are resilient, we develop a sense of confidence in our ability to navigate challenging situations, which can help us feel less helpless and more empowered. This can be particularly important when it comes to loneliness, as individuals who feel confident in their ability to cope with difficult emotions may be better able to take steps to connect with others and build meaningful relationships.

Resilience can also help curb loneliness by encouraging individuals to take an active role in seeking out social connections. Resilient individuals are often proactive and resourceful and may be more likely to take steps to build social support networks. This can involve reaching out to friends and family, joining social clubs or groups, or volunteering in the community. By taking an active role in seeking out social connections, individuals can build meaningful relationships that help curb feelings of loneliness.

Key Takeaway

Resilience can play an important role in curbing loneliness by fostering a sense of self-efficacy and encouraging individuals to take an active role in seeking out social connections. By building confidence in their ability to navigate challenging situations and taking proactive steps to connect with others, individuals can overcome feelings of isolation and loneliness and build stronger, more fulfilling relationships.

How are nature and resilience comparable?

Nature and resilience share many similarities, as both involve the ability to adapt and overcome challenges. Nature is a powerful force that is constantly adapting and evolving to changing circumstances, and resilience involves developing skills and abilities that allow us to do the same.

One way that nature and resilience are comparable is in their ability to withstand adversity. Just as nature is able to withstand extreme weather conditions, natural disasters, and other challenges, resilient individuals are able to cope with difficult situations and bounce back from setbacks. This involves developing skills such as emotional regulation, problem-solving, and perseverance, which allow individuals to adapt to changing circumstances and overcome obstacles.

Another way that nature and resilience are comparable is in their ability to grow and thrive in challenging environments. Many plants and animals are able to thrive in harsh and inhospitable environments, adapting to the unique challenges of their surroundings. Similarly, resilient individuals are able to grow and develop in the face of adversity, using challenges as opportunities for learning and personal growth.

Finally, both nature and resilience involve a sense of interconnectedness and interdependence. In nature, every organism is connected to its environment and dependent on the other organisms around it. Similarly, resilient individuals often rely on the support and encouragement of others in order to cope with difficult situations and build resilience. By recognizing our interdependence and seeking support from others, we can build the resilience we need to overcome life's challenges.

Key Takeaway

Nature and resilience are comparable in their ability to withstand adversity, grow and thrive in challenging environments, and recognize the importance of interconnectedness and interdependence. By learning from the resilience of nature and cultivating our own resilience, we can adapt to changing circumstances, overcome challenges, and achieve personal growth and development.

Chapter 8
Resilience: Individual, Teams, Organization, and Community

How is resilience developed at an individual level?

In the dynamics of life, resilience emerges not as an innate trait but as a skill that can be intentionally cultivated at an individual level. The journey toward resilience is marked by deliberate efforts and practices that empower individuals to confront life's challenges with strength and adaptability.

Building a robust support system, encompassing family, friends, or professional guidance, provides a foundation of interconnectedness that bolsters one's ability to navigate stress and adversity. The cultivation of a positive mindset becomes a transformative force, enabling individuals to perceive challenges as opportunities for growth and learning.

Embracing self-care as a non-negotiable practice fosters holistic well-being, while the art of setting realistic goals instills a sense of accomplishment and control. Resilience flourishes when individuals embrace adaptability, acknowledging that flexibility in the face of change is not a sign of vulnerability but a testament to strength.

Reflecting on past experiences becomes a poignant teacher, offering insights into effective coping strategies and shaping the trajectory of resilience. Through intentional and mindful steps, individuals embark on a journey to develop resilience, transforming life's trials into catalysts for personal growth and unwavering strength.

Resilience can be developed on an individual level through intentional effort and practice. Here are some ways that individuals can develop resilience:

Build a support system: Having a strong support system, such as family, friends, or a therapist, can help individuals cope with stress and overcome challenges. By building and maintaining strong relationships, individuals can develop a sense of connection and belonging, which can help them feel more resilient in the face of adversity.

Cultivate a positive mindset: A positive mindset can help individuals reframe challenges as opportunities for growth and learning. By focusing on their strengths and finding meaning in difficult situations, individuals can develop a sense of optimism and hope that can help them cope with adversity.

Practice self-care: Self-care is essential for maintaining physical, emotional, and mental well-being. By practicing self-care regularly, individuals can build their resilience by improving their overall health and well-being.

Set realistic goals: Setting realistic goals can help individuals build their confidence and sense of control. By breaking down larger goals into smaller, achievable steps, individuals can develop a sense of progress and accomplishment, which can help them feel more resilient.

Practice adaptability: Being adaptable and flexible in the face of change and uncertainty is a key component of resilience. By practicing adaptability regularly, individuals can build their capacity to handle unexpected challenges and changes in their lives.

Learn from past experiences: Reflecting on past experiences and identifying what worked and what didn't, can help individuals build their resilience by learning from their mistakes and identifying effective coping strategies for future challenges.

Key Takeaway

Developing resilience on an individual level involves building a support system, cultivating a positive mindset, practicing self-care, setting realistic goals, practicing adaptability, and learning from past experiences. By intentionally focusing on these areas, individuals can build their capacity to cope with stress and overcome challenges.

How is resilience developed in leaders to nurture teams and foster strength? Resilience is a cornerstone of effective leadership, particularly in environments where teams are developed and thrive. Leaders play a pivotal role not only in steering their teams toward success but also in cultivating a resilient mindset that can weather the storms of uncertainty and change. One key avenue for developing resilience as a leader is through the creation of a supportive team culture. Establishing an environment where open communication, trust, and collaboration flourish empowers team members to collectively navigate challenges. A leader's ability to foster a sense of camaraderie, where individuals feel heard and valued, strengthens the team's resilience as a whole.

Furthermore, resilience in leadership is intricately tied to adaptability. Leaders who embrace change and encourage their teams to view disruptions as opportunities for growth contribute significantly to the development of a resilient mindset. This involves creating a culture that views setbacks not as failures but as stepping stones toward improvement. Leaders who model adaptability in their decision-making and problem-solving processes inspire their teams to approach challenges with a flexible and proactive mindset.

Training and professional development programs tailored to resilience-building skills can also be instrumental. These programs can encompass stress management, emotional intelligence, and effective communication, providing leaders with the tools to navigate the complexities of team dynamics with resilience. Additionally, mentorship and coaching can offer valuable insights and guidance, allowing leaders to learn from the experiences of seasoned professionals and refine their own approaches to adversity.

Lastly, self-awareness is a linchpin in the development of resilience for leaders. Understanding one's strengths and areas for growth, coupled with a commitment to continuous self-improvement, lays the foundation for resilient leadership. This self-awareness extends to recognizing the well-being of team members, fostering a supportive environment where individuals are encouraged to prioritize their mental health and work-life balance.

In essence, resilience is not merely a quality possessed by leaders but a dynamic skill that can be nurtured and cultivated within the fabric of team development. As leaders invest in building resilient cultures, both individually and collectively, they fortify their teams to face challenges head-on, adapt to change, and emerge stronger, united, and ready for the complexities of the professional landscape.

Key Takeaway

Crucially, resilience in leadership intertwines with adaptability. Leaders championing change as a catalyst for growth instill a culture that views setbacks as opportunities for improvement. Modeling adaptability inspires flexible, proactive team responses to challenges. Tailored training programs in stress management, emotional intelligence, and effective communication equip leaders with the tools needed for resilient team dynamics. Mentorship and coaching add valuable perspectives, refining leaders' approaches to adversity.

How is resilience developed at an organizational level?

Resilience isn't solely an individual trait; it is a quality that thriving organizations can intentionally cultivate. Organizations, much like individuals, can navigate challenges more effectively when equipped with resilient frameworks. Creating a resilient organizational culture involves prioritizing values that foster positivity, strong interpersonal relationships, open communication, and continuous employee development. Encouraging adaptability is paramount, requiring initiatives like regular training programs, the promotion of a growth mindset, and a willingness to embrace innovation.

Employee well-being becomes a cornerstone, necessitating comprehensive support for physical, emotional, and mental health, and an acknowledgment of employee contributions. Developing crisis management plans ensures preparedness for unexpected hurdles, involving risk identification, contingency planning, and regular crisis drills. Collaboration and teamwork emerge as vital components, emphasizing cross-functional collaboration, diverse team building, and open communication. Learning from past experiences, acknowledging missteps, and identifying effective coping strategies completes the organizational resilience blueprint, positioning it to weather uncertainties and thrive in dynamic environments.

Resilience can also be developed on an organizational level through intentional effort and practice. Here are some ways that organizations can develop resilience:

Foster a culture of resilience: An organization that prioritizes resilience as a core value is more likely to develop a resilient workforce. This can be achieved by promoting a positive work environment, building strong relationships between colleagues, encouraging open communication and transparency, and investing in employee development.

Encourage adaptability: Encouraging adaptability and flexibility in the face of change and uncertainty is essential for developing organizational resilience. This can involve regular training and development programs, promoting a growth mindset, and embracing innovation and experimentation.

Invest in employee well-being: Employee well-being is essential for developing a resilient workforce. This can involve providing resources and support for physical, emotional, and mental health, promoting work-life balance, and recognizing and rewarding employee contributions.

Develop crisis management plans: Developing crisis management plans can help organizations prepare for unexpected challenges and emergencies. This can involve identifying potential risks, developing contingency plans, and conducting regular crisis drills and simulations.

Foster collaboration and teamwork: Collaboration and teamwork are essential for developing a resilient organization. This can involve promoting cross-functional collaboration, building diverse teams, and encouraging open communication and collaboration between team members.

Learn from past experiences: Reflecting on past experiences and identifying what worked and what didn't, can help organizations build their resilience by learning from their mistakes and identifying effective coping strategies for future challenges.

Key Takeaway

Developing resilience on an organizational level involves fostering a culture of resilience, encouraging adaptability, investing in employee well-being, developing crisis management plans, fostering collaboration and teamwork, and learning from past experiences. By intentionally focusing on these areas, organizations can build their capacity to cope with stress and overcome challenges.

How does engagement create resilience at the organizational level?

At the organizational level, the relationship between engagement and resilience is a dynamic force that shapes the very fabric of success. Employee engagement, characterized by a deep emotional connection to the work and the organization's mission, emerges as a linchpin for building resilience in the face of challenges.

When employees are not merely participants but enthusiastic contributors, the organizational landscape transforms. This transformation encompasses heightened motivation and commitment, fostering a workforce willing to navigate challenges with unwavering dedication. The adaptability and flexibility of engaged employees become organizational assets, enabling swift responses to change and disruptions.

Furthermore, a culture of collaboration and teamwork emerges, creating an environment where resilience thrives on collective efforts, diverse perspectives, and shared accountability. The psychological well-being of engaged employees forms a foundation for resilience, as satisfied and supported individuals are better equipped to withstand adversity.

Knowledge sharing and continuous learning become ingrained in the organizational culture, fortifying its adaptive capacity. Lastly, the ripple effects of engagement extend to talent management, with higher retention rates and increased attractiveness to skilled professionals, solidifying the organization's resilience in a competitive landscape.

In essence, engagement serves as the cornerstone upon which organizational resilience is not only built but continuously fortified.

Engagement plays a crucial role in creating resilience at the organization level. When employees are engaged, they are emotionally connected and invested in their work and the success of the organization. This high level of engagement leads to several factors that contribute to organizational resilience:

Motivation and commitment: Engaged employees are motivated to go above and beyond their basic job requirements. They are committed to the organization's goals and are willing to put in extra effort to achieve them. This motivation and commitment drive resilience by ensuring that employees remain focused and dedicated during challenging times.

Adaptability and flexibility: Engaged employees are more adaptable and flexible in the face of change. They are open to new ideas, receptive to feedback, and willing to learn and develop new skills. This adaptability allows organizations to respond effectively to unexpected events or disruptions, adjusting their strategies and operations to overcome challenges.

Collaboration and teamwork: Engaged employees are more likely to collaborate and work effectively as a team. They have a sense of ownership and accountability, fostering a supportive and cooperative work environment. This collaboration enables organizations to leverage diverse perspectives, skills, and experiences, leading to better problem-solving, innovation, and resilience.

Psychological well-being: Engagement is closely linked to employee well-being. Engaged employees experience higher job satisfaction, lower stress levels, and greater overall psychological well-being. When employees are well-supported and their well-being is prioritized, they are better equipped to cope with adversity and bounce back from setbacks, enhancing organizational resilience.

Knowledge sharing and learning: Engaged employees are eager to share their knowledge and contribute to the collective learning of the organization. They actively seek opportunities to develop new skills and stay updated with industry trends. This culture of knowledge sharing and continuous learning strengthens the organization's capacity to adapt, innovate, and remain resilient in the face of evolving challenges.

Retention and talent attraction: Organizations with high levels of engagement tend to have lower turnover rates and are more attractive to top talent. Engaged employees are more likely to stay with the organization during difficult times, ensuring continuity and preserving institutional knowledge. Additionally, organizations with a reputation for employee engagement are better positioned to attract and retain skilled individuals, further enhancing resilience.

Key Takeaway
Overall, engagement fosters a positive work environment, aligns employees with the organization's mission, and enhances their well-being and motivation. These factors combine to create a resilient organization that can navigate challenges, embrace change, and thrive in an ever-changing business landscape.

How is resilience developed at the Community Level?

Resilience at the community level is a collective endeavor, an interwoven collage of values, support systems, and adaptive capacities that enable individuals to weather storms, overcome challenges, and thrive in the face of adversity. Developing resilience within a community involves fostering a sense of connectedness, building social cohesion, and equipping individuals with the tools to navigate uncertainties. A resilient community is characterized by its ability to come together, support one another, and adapt in the aftermath of crises. Here are key strategies for developing resilience at the community level:

1. Community Engagement and Empowerment

Community Participation: Actively involving community members in decision-making processes empowers individuals and strengthens their sense of agency. Engaged communities are better equipped to respond collectively to challenges.

Skill Building: Providing opportunities for skill development, such as training in disaster preparedness or community organizing, enhances the community's ability to proactively address and mitigate potential risks.

2. Social Support Networks

Building Strong Relationships: Encouraging the development of social support networks within the community fosters a sense of belonging and provides a safety net during challenging times.

Community Organizations: Supporting and strengthening community organizations, such as local nonprofits and grassroots initiatives, can enhance the community's ability to mobilize resources and respond to crises effectively.

3. Effective Communication and Information Sharing

Open Communication Channels: Establishing transparent communication channels within the community ensures that information is disseminated quickly and accurately during emergencies, enabling prompt responses.

Education and Awareness: Promoting education and awareness campaigns on various topics, including disaster preparedness, health, and safety, equips community members with essential knowledge for resilience.

4. Infrastructure and Environmental Planning

Sustainable Infrastructure: Investing in resilient infrastructure, such as well-designed buildings and reliable communication systems, prepares communities for potential disruptions and minimizes the impact of disasters.

Environmental Stewardship: Encouraging environmentally sustainable practices and conservation efforts contributes to long-term resilience by safeguarding natural resources.

5. Crisis Response and Recovery Plans

Collaborative Planning: Developing comprehensive crisis response and recovery plans in collaboration with community members ensures that strategies are well-tailored to local needs and realities.

Mock Drills and Simulations: Conducting regular mock drills and simulations helps community members familiarize themselves with emergency procedures, enhancing their preparedness and resilience.

6. Cultural Preservation and Identity

Cultural Resilience: Embracing and preserving cultural practices and traditions fosters a sense of identity and resilience. Cultural continuity becomes a source of strength during challenging times.

Community Celebrations: Organizing events and celebrations that bring community members together promotes unity and reinforces a shared sense of purpose and resilience.

7. Access to Mental Health Services

Mental Health Support: Providing accessible mental health services and resources ensures that community members have the support needed to cope with the emotional toll of challenges and crises.

Community-Based Counseling: Implementing community-based counseling programs normalizes seeking mental health support and reduces stigma.

Developing resilience at the community level is an ongoing process that requires collaboration, commitment, and a deep understanding of the unique strengths and challenges of each community. By fostering a culture of empowerment, collaboration, and preparedness, communities can navigate uncertainties, support one another, and emerge stronger in the face of adversity.

Key Takeaway

Building resilience at the community level is a mosaic of interconnected strategies, emphasizing the importance of community engagement, social support networks, effective communication, and comprehensive planning. By actively involving members in decision-making processes, fostering strong relationships, and supporting community organizations, a resilient foundation is laid.

Transparent communication channels, education campaigns, and sustainable infrastructure contribute to preparedness, while crisis response plans, cultural preservation, and access to mental health services ensure adaptive capacities. Through these strategies, communities forge a collective identity, celebrate unity, and emerge stronger, fortified against the challenges that may arise.

In essence, community resilience is not just a response to adversity but a proactive, ongoing journey of empowerment and collaboration.

In conclusion, resilience as a leadership model offers valuable insights into developing the capacity to navigate challenges, bounce back from setbacks, and thrive in an ever-changing world. Resilience is essential for leaders at all levels, from individual contributors to organizational executives. It encompasses a range of qualities, skills, and perspectives that enable individuals and organizations to adapt, grow, and maintain their well-being in the face of adversity. By investing in resilience development, individuals can enhance their leadership effectiveness, help teams develop resilience, foster a culture of resilience within their organizations, and communities while contributing to their own growth and success.

The who is YOU, the what is RESILIENCE, the when is NOW, the where is EVERYWHERE, the why is to be a RESILIENT LEADER, the how is through this SELF- DEVELOPMENT BOOK!

Part II Wrap-up and Key Takeaways Summary

Resilience as a leadership model offers valuable insights into developing the capacity to navigate challenges, uncertainties, and setbacks effectively. It provides a roadmap for leaders to cultivate resilience within themselves and their organizations, enabling them to thrive in an ever-changing world.

Resilient leaders are individuals who recognize the importance of developing their resilience and actively seek to embody resilient qualities. They understand that resilience is not just about bouncing back from adversity but also about adapting, growing, and thriving in the face of challenges. Resilient leaders are driven by a desire to lead themselves and their teams with strength, agility, and the ability to overcome obstacles.

Resilience, in essence, is the ability to recover, adapt, and grow stronger from difficult experiences. It encompasses mental, emotional, and psychological fortitude. Resilience involves maintaining a positive outlook, staying grounded in the face of uncertainty, and being able to regulate one's emotions effectively. It is the capacity to persevere, problem-solve, and maintain focus in the midst of adversity.

Several factors impact the development of resilience. Personal experiences, such as facing adversity, setbacks, or trauma, can be catalysts for resilience development. Supportive relationships, a strong social network, and access to resources also play a vital role. Additionally, individual characteristics, such as self-awareness, optimism, and adaptability, contribute to the development of resilience.

The key tools of a resilient leader include self-awareness, emotional intelligence, adaptability, effective communication, and problem-solving skills. Resilient leaders are skilled at managing their own emotions and those of others. They have the ability to navigate change and uncertainty, make informed decisions, and rally their teams during challenging times.

Developing resilience requires a survival guide that entails various strategies and practices. This guide includes cultivating a growth mindset, building a support network, practicing self-care, maintaining perspective, and seeking continuous learning and growth. Resilient leaders are proactive in developing their resilience by embracing these strategies and incorporating them into their leadership approach.

Mental fragmentation refers to a state of psychological disarray, where thoughts, emotions, and actions become fragmented and disconnected. Resilience relates to mental fragmentation by providing a framework for integrating and regaining coherence during times of adversity. Resilient leaders possess the ability to maintain mental clarity, focus, and cohesion, even when faced with challenging circumstances.

Resilient leaders are needed in teams or organizations when there is a need for adaptability, problem-solving, and maintaining productivity in the face of disruptions or uncertainties. They provide stability, inspiration, and guidance during turbulent times. Resilient leaders foster a culture of resilience, where individuals feel supported, empowered, and equipped to navigate challenges and contribute their best efforts.

A leader becomes a resilient leader when they have developed the necessary skills, attitudes, and behaviors to navigate adversity effectively. They exhibit resilience in their decision-making, problem-solving, and communication. Resilient leaders inspire and motivate others, promote a positive and growth-oriented mindset, and foster an environment of trust, collaboration, and continuous learning.

Resilient leaders are most needed in environments where change, volatility, and ambiguity are prevalent. Industries and sectors undergoing rapid transformations, such as technology, healthcare, or global markets, require leaders who can navigate uncertainty and make informed decisions. Resilient leaders are also vital in times of crisis or disruption, where their ability to lead with clarity, compassion, and adaptability becomes critical.

However, there are instances where resilient leaders may not be needed, such as in stable or predictable environments where change is minimal. In such cases, other leadership qualities may be prioritized, such as consistency, reliability, or specialized expertise.

Resilience is important to those in leadership roles because it enables them to effectively lead through challenging situations, inspire and support their teams, and drive organizational success. Resilient leaders can maintain composure, make informed decisions, and adapt their strategies in the face of adversity. They model resilience for their teams and create a culture that fosters growth, innovation, and collective resilience.

Grit is a component of resilience development. It refers to the perseverance and passion for long-term goals, combined with the ability to maintain effort and resilience in the face of setbacks. Grit plays a role in developing resilience by fostering the determination and mental strength needed to overcome challenges and maintain focus on long-term objectives.

Grit and mental toughness are often used interchangeably, but they are not exactly the same thing. While both concepts involve perseverance and resilience, mental toughness tends to focus more on endurance, competitive spirit, and pushing through difficult circumstances. Grit, on the other hand, emphasizes passion, consistency, and maintaining effort towards long-term goals. While closely related, they have slightly different emphases within the context of resilience development.

Resilience and mental toughness are related, but resilience encompasses a broader spectrum of qualities and skills. Resilience involves the ability to adapt, bounce back from setbacks, and maintain overall well-being in the face of adversity. Mental toughness, on the other hand, primarily focuses on endurance, persistence, and the ability to perform under pressure. Resilience includes mental toughness as a component but also incorporates emotional intelligence, adaptability, and other skills essential for navigating challenges effectively.

Resilience applies to psychological trauma by offering a framework for individuals to recover, heal, and rebuild their lives after experiencing trauma. Resilience helps individuals maintain their psychological well-being, adapt to new circumstances, and regain a sense of control and meaning in their lives. It involves developing coping mechanisms, seeking support, and engaging in self-care practices to navigate the emotional and psychological impacts of trauma.

Resilience is crucial in states of uncertainty because it enables individuals and leaders to navigate ambiguity, make informed decisions, and maintain focus and effectiveness. Resilience helps individuals manage their emotions, stay adaptable, and maintain a positive mindset in the face of uncertainty. It allows leaders to guide their teams through uncertain times, provide clarity and stability, and foster an environment of trust and collaboration.

Hope is an integral part of resilience as it provides individuals with a positive outlook, a belief in the possibility of a better future, and the motivation to persevere through challenges. Hope fuels resilience by instilling optimism, determination, and a sense of purpose. It allows individuals to see beyond their present circumstances and envision a brighter outcome.

Resilience helps individuals overcome hardships by providing them with the inner strength, coping mechanisms, and adaptive strategies to navigate and transcend difficult experiences. Resilience enables individuals to bounce back from setbacks, learn from failures, and find new ways forward. It allows individuals to draw on their resources, inner reserves, and support networks to overcome obstacles and emerge stronger.

Resilience helps establish a new normal by facilitating adaptation, growth, and the ability to embrace change. In times of significant disruptions or transitions, resilience enables individuals to adjust their mindset, behaviors, and strategies to align with the new reality. It helps individuals let go of what was and embrace what can be, paving the way for the creation of a new normal.

Resilience negates fear by providing individuals with the tools and mindset to confront and manage fear effectively. Resilient individuals develop the capacity to regulate their emotions, challenge limiting beliefs, and face their fears head-on. Resilience allows individuals to cultivate courage, embrace discomfort, and navigate challenges with a sense of confidence and calm.

Resilience and nourishing the soul are related in the sense that resilience extends beyond the surface-level challenges and encompasses a deeper level of well-being and fulfillment. Nourishing the soul involves attending to one's spiritual, emotional, and psychological needs, which are essential for building resilience. Resilient individuals recognize the importance of self-care, finding meaning and purpose, and cultivating a sense of connection and alignment with their values and beliefs.

The act of suffering can contribute to the development of resilience by challenging individuals, forcing them to confront their limitations, and building their capacity to endure and overcome adversity. Through suffering, individuals can tap into their inner strength, discover their resilience, and develop the skills and perspectives necessary to navigate future challenges.

The reserves of resilience sustain an individual by providing a reservoir of inner strength, coping mechanisms, and adaptive strategies to draw upon during difficult times. Resilience allows individuals to endure, persevere, and maintain their well-being and effectiveness even in the face of prolonged or recurring challenges. It offers a source of psychological and emotional support that helps individuals weather storms and emerge stronger.

Trauma can build on more trauma when individuals are repeatedly exposed to distressing or overwhelming experiences without sufficient support or opportunities for recovery. Unresolved trauma can compound and intensify the challenges individuals face, making resilience development more complex. However, resilience also offers a pathway for healing, growth, and the restoration of well-being in the aftermath of trauma.

Resilience is closely related to well-being as it contributes to individuals' ability to maintain balance, cope with stress, and sustain their mental and emotional health. Resilient individuals are better equipped to navigate challenges, maintain positive relationships, and cultivate a sense of purpose and fulfillment. By investing in resilience, individuals enhance their overall well-being and quality of life.

Structure and routine play a significant role in building resilience by providing stability, predictability, and a sense of control in individuals' lives. Engaging in structured activities, maintaining healthy habits, and establishing routines can help individuals manage stress, regulate emotions, and maintain a sense of normalcy even in the face of disruptions or uncertainties. Structure and routine contribute to building resilience by promoting stability, fostering self-discipline, and enabling individuals to navigate challenges more effectively.

Building resilience equals unparalleled times of self-growth because it requires individuals to confront their limitations, adapt to new circumstances, and develop new skills and perspectives. The process of building resilience often involves stepping outside of one's comfort zone, embracing discomfort, and challenging oneself to grow. Through this journey, individuals discover their inner strength, develop new capacities, and cultivate a deeper understanding of themselves and the world around them.

Spiritual convictions ground resilience by providing individuals with a sense of purpose, meaning, and a broader perspective on life. Spiritual beliefs and practices offer a framework for understanding and making sense of difficult experiences. They can provide comfort, hope, and a source of inner strength during challenging times. Resilience is deeply intertwined with spirituality, as it draws upon the individual's values, faith, and connection to something greater than themselves.

Loneliness can be curbed with resilience as resilient individuals develop the skills and resources to seek support, cultivate connections, and navigate feelings of isolation. Resilience enables individuals to maintain a sense of belonging, foster meaningful relationships, and find support networks during challenging times. By building resilience, individuals can combat loneliness and cultivate a sense of connection and community.

Nature and resilience share similarities in the sense that they both have the power to restore, rejuvenate, and inspire. Spending time in nature can have a positive impact on mental well-being, reduce stress, and promote resilience. Nature provides individuals with a sense of awe, connection, and perspective that can contribute to their ability to bounce back from challenges and maintain a positive outlook.

Resilience is developed at an individual level through a combination of self-reflection, self-awareness, self-care, and continuous learning. Individuals can cultivate resilience by developing a growth mindset, building emotional intelligence, practicing self-compassion, seeking support, and adopting adaptive coping strategies. It requires a commitment to personal growth, embracing challenges as opportunities, and developing the skills and perspectives necessary to navigate adversity effectively.

Resilience is also developed at an organizational level through fostering a culture that values adaptability, learning, and collaboration. Organizations can promote resilience by providing resources and support for employee well-being, encouraging innovation and creativity, and creating an environment where failures are viewed as learning opportunities. Developing resilient organizations involves empowering employees, building strong teams, and fostering a culture of psychological safety and continuous improvement.

Engagement plays a crucial role in creating resilience at the organizational level. When employees feel engaged, connected, and valued, they are more likely to demonstrate resilience in the face of challenges. Engaged employees are motivated, committed, and have a sense of ownership in their work. Organizations can foster engagement by providing opportunities for growth, meaningful work, and promoting a positive and inclusive work environment.

Key Takeaways Summary

Resilience Leadership Model

1. Resilience as a leadership model involves cultivating self-awareness, adaptability, a positive mindset, effective communication, relationship-building, decision-making under pressure, a learning orientation, emotional intelligence, and well-being. By embodying these qualities and applying these strategies, leaders can foster resilience within themselves and their organizations, guiding them towards success in the face of adversity.

2. Anyone who wants to be an effective leader would benefit from becoming a resilient leader, as resilience is essential for navigating the many challenges that leaders face in today's fast-paced and complex environment.

3. Resilience is the ability to adapt and recover from difficult or stressful situations. Leaders can develop resilience through a combination of mindset, self-care, skill-building, and learning from experience. By building resilience, leaders are better equipped to navigate challenges and uncertainty, and to continue to achieve their goals despite setbacks.

4. There are several other factors that can impact resilience development for leaders, including social support, emotional intelligence, flexibility, and a sense of purpose and meaning. By cultivating these factors, leaders can enhance their ability to adapt and recover from difficult situations, and to maintain a positive outlook even in the face of adversity.

5. The key tools of a resilient leader include self-awareness, emotional intelligence, adaptability, positive mindset, proactive problem-solving,

support network, and self-care. By developing these tools, leaders can enhance their ability to navigate challenges and maintain their focus and effectiveness over the long term.

6. Developing resilience involves building skills, attitudes, and behaviors that allow individuals to adapt and bounce back from difficult situations. By building strong relationships, cultivating a positive mindset, practicing self-care, setting realistic goals, building problem-solving skills, learning from challenges, and seeking out support, individuals can develop resilience and thrive in the face of adversity.

7. Mental fragmentation is a complex and challenging experience that can have significant impacts on an individual's mental and emotional well-being. With appropriate treatment and support, however, it may be possible to recover a sense of coherence and continuity in one's thoughts, feelings, and sense of self, and to promote healing and recovery from trauma.

8. Resilient leaders are needed in teams or organizations when facing challenges, uncertainties, or changes that require strong leadership to navigate. They are able to provide stability, direction, and support to their team, and adapt to changing circumstances to ensure the success of the team or organization.

9. A leader becomes a resilient leader when they are able to navigate difficult situations with grace and composure, while inspiring their teams to do the same. Developing resilience takes time and effort and the journey is not a one fits all path.

10. Resilient leaders are needed in every industry, but particularly in industries where the challenges are significant and the need for adaptability and agility is high. Resilient leaders play a critical role across diverse industries, offering stability in the face of uncertainty and guiding teams

through challenges. In healthcare, where high stress and rapid decision-making are constants, resilient leaders ensure the well-being of both teams and patients. The technology sector demands leaders capable of navigating constant evolution, while resilient leaders in finance manage market volatility and economic uncertainty. In education, marked by perpetual change, resilient leaders adapt to evolving circumstances for the benefit of students. Nonprofit organizations, facing unique challenges, rely on resilient leaders to navigate complexities and steer toward mission-driven goals. While resilience is universally valuable, it proves particularly crucial in industries where unpredictability is inherent, ensuring sustained success and fostering growth.

11. Resilience is important to those in leadership roles because it helps them to deal with challenges, cope with stress, build trust, model behavior, and achieve goals. By developing resilience, leaders can enhance their ability to lead effectively and to achieve long-term success for themselves and their organizations.

12. Grit is a key component of resilience development, as it involves the ability to persevere in the face of adversity and to maintain a long-term goal despite setbacks. Leaders can develop grit by developing a growth mindset, building perseverance, developing resilience, and learning from experience. By building grit, leaders are better equipped to maintain their focus and persistence, they keep going, even in the face of significant challenges.

13. While mental toughness and grit share some similarities, they are not the same thing. Both mental toughness and grit can be important traits for leaders, and developing both can help leaders to maintain their focus, persistence, and resilience in the face of challenges and setbacks.

The Mind, Emotions, and Resilience

14. Resilience plays a crucial role in helping individuals recover from psychological trauma. It allows individuals to adapt to the challenges of trauma and develop the skills and strategies necessary to cope, recover, and move forward in their lives.

15. Resilience can help individuals to cope with states of uncertainty by allowing them to regulate their emotions and thoughts, remain adaptable and flexible, seek out information and support, engage in problem-solving behaviors, and find meaning and purpose in their lives.

16. Hope is an essential part of resilience. It provides individuals with a sense of purpose and direction, a sense of agency and control, and a sense of connection and support. By cultivating hope, individuals can build their resilience and bounce back from difficult situations.

17. Resilience helps individuals to overcome hardships by allowing them to regulate their emotions and thoughts, seek out support and resources, find meaning and purpose in their experiences, and maintain a positive outlook. By building resilience, individuals can become better equipped to overcome the challenges that life throws their way.

18. Resilience can help individuals establish a new normal by allowing them to regulate their emotions and thoughts, be flexible and adaptable, find meaning and purpose, and maintain a positive outlook. By building resilience, individuals can adapt to change and create a new normal that allows them to thrive.

19. Resilience does not negate fear, but it can help individuals to manage and cope with fear more effectively, which can reduce its negative impact on their lives.

20. While suffering can be a challenging and painful experience, it can also provide an opportunity for individuals to develop resilience and other important life skills. By learning to cope with adversity, individuals can become more capable of managing future challenges, and can cultivate a greater sense of well-being and purpose in their lives.

21. By cultivating and maintaining these reserves of resilience, individuals can build their capacity to cope with adversity and recover from stress or trauma. This can help to promote overall well-being and can contribute to a sense of inner strength and resilience that can support individuals throughout their lives. Resilience has reserves and can sustain an individual for a long time but when the reserves are exhausted the individual will desire or require a change.

22. Trauma can build on more trauma through a complex interplay of psychological, behavioral, social, and environmental factors. By understanding the trauma cascade and the ways in which trauma can impact an individual's life, it may be possible to develop more effective interventions and supports to break the cycle of trauma and promote healing and resilience.

23. Resilience is closely related to well-being, as it can support mental and physical health, enhance life satisfaction, and promote social connections. By developing and maintaining resilience, individuals can cultivate a greater sense of well-being and resilience in the face of adversity.

24. Having structure in our lives can help us build resilience by providing a sense of predictability, purpose, good habits, and support. By developing these skills, we can better manage stress and adversity and bounce back from difficult situations.

25. Spiritual convictions can ground resilience by providing a sense of perspective, comfort, and community. By connecting with a larger purpose

or plan, finding solace in spiritual practices, and connecting with others who share our beliefs, we can find the strength and determination to persevere through difficult times.

26. Resilience can play an important role in curbing loneliness by fostering a sense of self-efficacy and encouraging individuals to take an active role in seeking out social connections. By building confidence in their ability to navigate challenging situations and taking proactive steps to connect with others, individuals can overcome feelings of isolation and loneliness and build stronger, more fulfilling relationships.

27. Nature and resilience are comparable in their ability to withstand adversity, grow and thrive in challenging environments, and recognize the importance of interconnectedness and interdependence. By learning from the resilience of nature and cultivating our own resilience, we can adapt to changing circumstances, overcome challenges, and achieve personal growth and development

28. Developing resilience on an individual level involves building a support system, cultivating a positive mindset, practicing self-care, setting realistic goals, practicing adaptability, and learning from past experiences. By intentionally focusing on these areas, individuals can build their capacity to cope with stress and overcome challenges.

29. Crucially, resilience in leadership intertwines with adaptability. Leaders championing change as a catalyst for growth instill a culture that views setbacks as opportunities for improvement. Modeling adaptability inspires flexible, proactive team responses to challenges. Tailored training programs in stress management, emotional intelligence, and effective communication equip leaders with the tools needed for resilient team dynamics. Mentorship and coaching add valuable perspectives, refining leaders' approaches to adversity.

30. Developing resilience on an organizational level involves fostering a culture of resilience, encouraging adaptability, investing in employee well-being, developing crisis management plans, fostering collaboration and teamwork, and learning from past experiences. By intentionally focusing on these areas, organizations can build their capacity to cope with stress and overcome challenges.

31. Engagement fosters a positive work environment, aligns employees with the organization's mission, and enhances their well-being and motivation. These factors combine to create a resilient organization that can navigate challenges, embrace change, and thrive in an ever-changing business landscape.

32. Building resilience at the community level is a mosaic of interconnected strategies, emphasizing the importance of community engagement, social support networks, effective communication, and comprehensive planning. By actively involving members in decision-making processes, fostering strong relationships, and supporting community organizations, a resilient foundation is laid.

Transparent communication channels, education campaigns, and sustainable infrastructure contribute to preparedness, while crisis response plans, cultural preservation, and access to mental health services ensure adaptive capacities. Through these strategies, communities forge a collective identity, celebrate unity, and emerge stronger, fortified against the challenges that may arise. In essence, community resilience is not just a response to adversity but a proactive, ongoing journey of empowerment and collaboration.

Resilient Leadership Conclusion

The topics explored in Book 1 of the *Resilient Leadership* series is to present a comprehensive exploration of resilient leadership and its various dimensions. Part I served as an introduction, setting the stage for understanding the significance of resilience in leadership roles. It highlighted the essential characteristics and qualities of resilient leaders and established the foundation for further exploration.

Part II delved into the intricacies of resilience, exploring the who, what, when, where, why, and how of resilience. It provided a holistic understanding of resilience, its sources, and manifestations in different contexts. This chapter emphasized the multifaceted nature of resilience and the importance of developing it at both individual and collective levels.

It is the purpose of Book 1 of this three-part series to provide a comprehensive framework for understanding and developing resilient leadership. The work underscores the importance of resilience in leadership roles, explored the threats that can impede its development, and provided practical strategies and insights to enhance resilience at individual, team, organizational, and community levels. By cultivating resilient leadership, individuals and organizations can navigate adversity, foster growth, and contribute to the well-being and success of their communities.

The Resilient Leader begins by cultivating personal resilience and then fosters a team of resilient leaders. These leaders, in turn, shape resilient organizations, creating communities where resilience is not only nurtured but becomes a cornerstone of collective strength and growth.

References

The Aftermath of Horror. (1917). Journal of *Education*, 86(22), 605.

Alderfer, C. P. (1972). *Existence, relatedness, and growth human needs in organizational settings.* The Free Press.

An Appalling Catastrophe. (1917). *Journal of Education*, 86(22), 605.

American Psychological Association. (n.d.a). Resilience. In APA Dictionary of Psychology. Retrieved June 9, 2022, from https://dictionary.apa.org/resilience

Arond-Thomas, M. (2004). Resilient leadership for challenging times. *Physician Executive*, 30(4), 18-21.

Bagshaw, M., & Bagshaw, C. (1999). Leadership in the twenty-first century. *Industrial & Commercial Training*, 31(6), 236. https://doi.org/10.1108/00197859910291414

Baker, D. P., Day, R., & Salas, E. (2006). Teamwork as an essential component of high-reliability organizations. *Health Services Research*, 41(4P2), 1576-1598. https://doi.org/10.1111/j.1475-6773.2006.00566.x

Bakker, A. B., Le Blanc, P. M., & Schaufeli, W. B. (2005). Burnout contagion among intensive care nurses. *Journal of Advanced Nursing (Wiley-Blackwell)*, 51(3), 276-287. https://doi.org/10.1111/j.1365-2648.2005.03494.x

Bass, B.M. (1985), "Leadership: good, better, best", *Organisational Dynamics*, pp. 26-40.

Blackwell, J. (2021, November 30). *Active 2021 Atlantic hurricane season officially ends: Reliable early NOAA forecasts helped safeguard communities.* Retrieved July 13, 2022, from https://www.noaa.gov/news-release/active-2021-atlantic-hurricane-season-officially-ends

Brown, L. M., Bruce, M. L., Hyer, K., Mills, W. L., Vongxaiburana, E., & Polivka-West, L. (2009). A pilot study evaluating the feasibility of psychological first aid for nursing home residents. *Clinical Gerontologist,* 32(3), 293-308. https://doi.org/10.1080/07317110902895317

Cho, E. & Cho, H. H. (2021). Factors influencing compassion fatigue among hospice and palliative care unit nurses. *Korean Journal of Hospice & Palliative Care,* 24(1), 13-25. https://doi.org/10.14475/jhpc.2021.24.1.13

Crosweller, M., & Tschakert, P. (2020). Disaster management leadership and policy making: a critical examination of communitarian and individualistic understandings of resilience and vulnerability. *Climate Policy (Taylor & Francis Ltd),* 1-19. https://doi.org/10.1080/14693062.2020.1833825

Cunningham, C. (2020). Survival of the fittest. In *Encyclopedia Britannica.* Retrieved June 22, 2022 from https://www.britannica.com/science/survival-of-the-fittest

Curran, C. R., & Fitzpatrick, T. A. (2014). Could this be the year to claim the corner office? *Nursing Economic$,* 32(1), 49-50.

Dartey-Baah, K. (2015). Resilient leadership: a transformational-transactional leadership mix. *Journal of Global Responsibility*, 6(1), 99-112. http://dx.doi.org/10.1108/JGR-07-2014-0026

Diddams, M., & Chang, G. C. (2012). Only human: Exploring the nature of weakness in authentic leadership. *The Leadership Quarterly*, 23(3), 593-603. https://doi.org/10.1016/j.leaqua.2011.12.010

Dimas, I. D., Rebelo, T., Lourenço, P. R., & Pessoa, C. I. P. (2018). Bouncing back from setbacks: On the mediating role of team resilience in the relationship between transformational leadership and team effectiveness. *Journal of Psychology*, 152(6), 358-372. https://www-tandfonline-com.radford.idm.oclc.org/doi/pdf/10.1080/00223980.2018.1465022

Dückers, M. L. A., Yzermans, C. J., Jong, W., & Boin, A. (2017). Psychosocial crisis management: The unexplored intersection of crisis leadership and psychosocial support. *Risk, Hazards & Crisis in Public Policy*, 8(2), 94-112. https://doi.org/10.1002/rhc3.12113

Dyer, J. G., & McGuinness, T. M. (1996). Resilience: analysis of the concept. *Archives of Psychiatric Nursing*, 10(5), 276-282. https://doi.org/10.1016/S0883-9417(96)80036-7

Eliot, J. L. (2020). Resilient leadership: The impact of a servant leader on the resilience of their followers. *Advances in Developing Human Resources*, 22(4), 404-418. https://doi.org/10.1177/1523422320945237

Eva, N., Robin, M., Sendjaya, S., van Dierendonck, D., & Liden, R. C. (2019). Servant leadership: A systematic review and call for future research. *The Leadership Quarterly*, 30(1), 111-132. https://doi.org/10.1016/j.leaqua.2018.07.004

Everly, Jr., G. S., McCabe, O. L., Semon, N. L., Thompson, C. B., & Links, J. M. (2014). The development of a model of psychological first aid for non-mental health trained public health personnel: The Johns Hopkins RAPID-PFA. *Journal of Public Health Management & Practice, 20*, S24-S29. https://doi.org/10.1097/PHH.0000000000000065

Everly, Jr.,, G. S., Smith, K. J., & Lobo, R. (2013). Resilient leadership and the organizational culture of resilience: Construct validation. *International Journal of Emergency Mental Health and Human Resilience, 15*(2), 123-128.

FEMA. (n.d.a). Disaster. In *Glossary*. Retrieved from June 24, 2022 from https://training.fema.gov/programs/emischool/el361toolkit/glossary.htm#C

FEMA. (n.d.b). Emergency. In *Glossary*. Retrieved from June 24, 2022 from https://training.fema.gov/programs/emischool/el361toolkit/glossary.htm#C

Fernandez, F., Coulson, H., & Zou, Y. (2022). Leading in the eye of a storm: how one team of administrators exercised disaster resilience. *Higher Education* (00181560), 83(4), 929-944. https://doi.org/10.1007/s10734-021-00716-5

Giustiniano, L., Pina e Cunha, M., Simpson, A. V., Rego, A., & Clegg, S. (2020). Resilient leadership as paradox work: Notes from COVID-19. *Management and Organization Review, 16*(5), 971-975. https://dx.doi.org/10.1017/mor.2020.57

Goleman, D. (2000). Leadership that gets results. *Harvard Business Review, 78*(2), 78-90.

Golper, L.A.C. (2009). Leadership: finding your inner Throgmartin. *Perspectives on Administration & Supervision*, 19(2), 39-44.

Grabbe, L., Higgins, M. K., Baird, M., Craven, P. A., & San Fratello, S. (2020). The Community Resiliency Model® to promote nurse well-being. *Nursing Outlook, 68*(3), 324-336. https://doi.org/10.1016/j.outlook.2019.11.002

Gwin, J. B. (1930). Do disasters help? *Social Forces,* 8(3), 386-389. https://doi.org/10.2307/2570182

Hitt, M. A., Miller, C. C., & Colella, A. (2015a). Content theories of motivation: Hierarchy of needs theory - ERG theory. In Johnson, L. (Ed.), *Organizational behavior* (4th ed.). (pp. 179-182). John Wiley and Sons.

Hitt, M. A., Miller, C. C., & Colella, A. (2015b). Organizational change and development: Planned change. In Johnson, L. (Ed.), *Organizational behavior* (4th ed.). (pp. 457-459). John Wiley and Sons.

Hosp, H. M. (1944). Education for women. *Educational Leadership,* 1(5), 288-291.

House, R. J., & Mitchell, T. R. (1975). *Path-goal theory of leadership.* Organizational Research (NI-25). https://apps.dtic.mil/sti/pdfs/ADA009513.pdf

Hutchins, H. M., & Wang, J. (2008). Organizational crisis management and human resource development: A review of the literature and implications to HRD research and practice. *Advances in Developing Human Resources,* 10(3), 310-330. https://doi.org/10.1177/1523422308316183

Hyer, K., Polivka-West, L., & Brown, L. M. (2007). Nursing homes and assisted living facilities: Planning and decision making for sheltering in place or evacuation. *Generations*, 31(4), 29-33.

Jun, J. (2020). Vicarious resilience: Cultivating internal strength through external support. *The American Journal of Nursing*, 120(11), 13. https://doi.org/10.1097/01.NAJ.0000721872.42520.2b

Kahn, M. J. & Sachs, B. P. (2018). Crises and turnaround management: Lessons learned from recovery of New Orleans and Tulane University following hurricane katrina. *Rambam Maimonides Medical Journal, 9* (4), e0031. https://doi.org/10.5041/RMMJ.10354

Kaminsky, M., McCabe, O. L., Langlieb, A. M., & Everly, G. S., Jr. (2007). An evidence-informed model of human resistance, resilience, and recovery: The Johns Hopkins' outcome-driven paradigm for disaster mental health services. *Brief Treatment and Crisis Intervention*, 7(1), 1-11. https://doi.org/10.1093/brief-treatment/mhl015

Kelsey, E. A., West, C. P., Cipriano, P. F., Peterson, C., Satele, D., Shanafelt, T., & Dyrbye, L. N. (2021). Original research: Suicidal ideation and attitudes toward help seeking in U.S. nurses relative to the general working population. *AJN American Journal of Nursing*, 121(11), 24-36. https://doi.org/10.1097/01.NAJ.0000798056.73563.fa

Khoo, T. C., Jesudason, E., & FitzGerald, A. (2021). Catching our breath: reshaping rehabilitation services for COVID-19. *Disability & Rehabilitation*, 43(1), 112-117. https://doi.org/10.1080/09638288.2020.1808905

King, A. S. (1990). Evolution of leadership theory. *Vikalpa*, 15(2), 43-54. https://doi.org/10.1177/0256090919900205

Kouze, J. M., & Posner, B. Z. (1999). *Encouraging the heart: A leader's guide to rewarding and recognizing others.* Jossey-Bass.

Kouze, J. M., & Posner, B. Z. (2003). *The leadership challenge* (3rd ed.). Jossey-Bass.

Kouze, J. M., & Posner, B. Z. (2007). *The leadership challenge* (4th ed.). John Wiley and Sons.

Ledlow, G. R., & Stephens, J. H. (2018). Chronology of leadership study and practice. In C. McAlister's (Ed.), *Leadership for health professionals: theory, skills, and applications* (3rd ed.), pp.61-94. Jones & Bartlett Learning.

Lewin, K. (1947). Frontiers in group dynamics: Concepts, method and reality in social sciences, social equilibria and social change. *Human Relations,* 1, 5-42.

Libuser CB. *Organization structure and risk mitigation.* Dissertation submitted in partial satisfaction of the requirements for the degree of Doctor of Philosophy in Management. Los Angeles: University of California, 1994.

Liu, H., & Boyatzis, R. E. (2021). Focusing on resilience and renewal from stress: The role of emotional and social intelligence competencies. *Frontiers in Psychology, 12.* https://doi.org/10.3389/fpsyg.2021.685829

Lugg, C. A., & Boyd, W. L. (1993). Leadership for collaboration: Reducing risk and fostering resilience. *The Phi Delta Kappan,* 75(3), 253-258.

Luthans, F., & Church, A. H. (2002). Positive organizational behavior: Developing and managing psychological strengths [and executive commentary]. *The Academy of Management Executive (1993-2005), 16* (1), 57-75.

Malakyan, P. G. (2014). Followership in leadership studies: A case of leader-follower trade approach. *Journal of Leadership Studies, 7* (4), 6-22. https://doi.org/10.1002/jls.21306

Maslow, A. H. (1943). A theory of human motivation. *Psychological Review,* 50(4), 370-396. https://doi.org/10.1037/h0054346

Masten, A. S. (2001). Ordinary magic: Resilience processes in development. *American Psychologist, 56* (3), 227-238. https://doi.org/10.1037//0003-066x.56.3.227

Mather LifeWays. (2012). *Mather LifeWays' "PREPARE" training program for healthcare workers.* Mather. https://www.mather.com/wp-content/uploads/2012/05/PREPAREU.S.Dept_.OfHomelandSecurity.pdf

McGarry, B. E., & Grabowski, D. C. (2021). Nursing homes and COVID-19: A crisis on top of a crisis. *The ANNALS of the American Academy of Political and Social Science, 698* (1), 137-162.

Merriam-Webster. (n.d.a). Crisis. In *Merriam-Webster.com dictionary.* Retrieved June 24, 2022, from https://www.merriam-webster.com/dictionary/crisis

Merriam-Webster. (n.d.b). Disruption. In *Merriam-Webster.com dictionary.* Retrieved June 24, 2022, from https://www.merriam-webster.com/dictionary/disruption

Merriam-Webster. (n.d.c). Disturbance. In *Merriam-Webster.com dictionary*. Retrieved June 24, 2002, from https://www.merriam-webster.com/dictionary/disturbance

Merriam-Webster. (n.d.d). Resilience. In *Merriam-Webster.com dictionary*. Retrieved May 29, 2022, from https://www.merriam-webster.com/dictionary/resilience

Mitroff, I., Shrivastava, P., & Udwadia, F. (1987). Effective crisis management. *Academy of Management Executive*. 1. 283-292. https://doi.org/10.5465/ame.1987.4275639

Moore, J. W. (2016). What is the sense of agency and why does it matter? *Frontiers in Psychology, 7*(1272). https://doi.org/10.3389/fpsyg.2016.01272

Norrish, B. R., & Rundall, T. G. (2001). Hospital restructuring and the work of registered nurses. *The Milbank Quarterly, 79*(1), 55-79. https://doi.org/10.1111/1468-0009.00196

Paine, K., & Prochnow, J. A. (2022). Leadership strategies to support resilience. *Nursing Management, 53*(4), 12-19. https://doi.org/10.1097/01.NUMA.0000824024.53750.66

Peterson, C., Sussell, A., Jia Li, Schumacher, P. K., Yeoman, K., Stone, D. M., & Li, J. (2020). Suicide rates by industry and occupation - national violent death reporting system, 32 states, 2016. *MMWR: Morbidity & Mortality Weekly Report, 69*(3), 57-62. https://doi.org/10.15585/mmwr.mm6903a1

Pols, H., & Oak, S. (2007). War & military mental health: The US psychiatric response in the 20th century. *American Journal of Public Health*, 97(12), 2132-2142. https://doi.org/10.2105/AJPH.2006.090910

Pring, E. T., Malietzis, G., Kendall, S. W. H., Jenkins, J. T., & Athanasiou, T. (2021). Crisis management for surgical teams and their leaders, lessons from the COVID-19 pandemic: A structured approach to developing resilience or natural organizational responses. *International Journal of Surgery, 91*. https://doi.org/10.1016/j.ijsu.2021.105987

Pulley, M. L. (1997). Leading resilient organizations. *Leadership in Action, 17*(4), 1-5.

Resnick, B. (2020). Covid-19 lessons learned from the voices of our geriatric nurses: Leadership, resilience, and heroism. *Geriatric Nursing, 41*(4), 357-359. https://doi.org/10.1016/j.gerinurse.2020.06.008

Richardson, G. E. (2002). The metatheory of resilience and resiliency. *Journal of Clinical Psychology, 58*(3), 307-321. https://doi.org/10.1002/jclp.10020

Roberts, K. H., Madsen, P., Desai, V., & Van Stralen, D. (2005). A case of the birth and death of a high reliability healthcare organisation. *BMJ Quality & Safety, 14*(3), 216-220. https://www.ncbi.nlm.nih.gov/pmc/articles/PMC1744010/pdf/v014p00216.pdf

Stajkovic, A. D., & Luthans, F. (1998). Social cognitive theory and self-efficacy: Going beyond traditional motivational and behavioral approaches. *Organizational Dynamics, 26*(4), 62-74. https://doi.org/10.1016/S0090-2616(98)90006-7

Teo, W.L., Lee, M., & Lim, W.S. (2017). The relational activation of resilience model: How leadership activates resilience in an organizational crisis. *Journal of Contingencies and Crisis Management, 25*(3), 136-147. https://doi.org/10.1111/1468-5973.12179

Thwaite, S. V. (2022). Crisis is a powerful teacher: Resilient leadership during a global health pandemic. *Journal of Leadership Education, 21* (1), 196-208. https://doi.org/10.12806/V21/I1/C1

Tsao, C. W., Aday, A. W., Almarzooq, Z. I., Alonso, A., Beaton, A. Z., Bittencourt, M. S., Boehme, A. K., Buxton, A. E., Carson, A. P., Commodore-Mensah, Y., Elkind, M. S. V., Evenson, K. R., Eze-Nliam, C., Ferguson, J. F., Generoso, G., Ho, J. E., Kalani, R., Khan, S. S., Kissela, B. M., ... Martin, S.S. (2022). Heart disease and stroke statistics-2022 update: A report from the American Heart Association. *Circulation, 145* (8), 1-487. https://doi-org.radford.idm.oclc.org/10.1161/CIR.0000000000001052

Tseng, H.-C., Chen, T.-F., & Chou, S.-M. (2005). SARS: Key factors in crisis management. *The Journal of Nursing Research: JNR, 13* (1), 58-65.

Tsuda, S., Olasky, J., & Jones, D. B. (2021). Team training and surgical crisis management. *Journal of surgical oncology, 124* (2), 216-220. https://doi.org/10.1002/jso.26523

United States Department of Health and Human Services (US-DHHS), Centers for Medicare and Medicaid Services (CMS). (2021, December 1). *Emergency Preparedness Rule*. CMS.gov. https://www.cms.gov/Medicare/Provider-Enrollment-and-Certification/SurveyCertEmergPrep/Emergency-Prep-Rule

United States Department of Homeland Security (US-DHS), Federal Emergency Management Agency (FEMA). (2011, September). *National Disaster Recovery Framework: Strengthening Disaster Recovery for the Nation*. https://www.fema.gov/pdf/recoveryframework/ndrf.pdf

United States Department of Homeland Security (US-DHS), Federal Emergency Management Agency (FEMA). (2019). *Publication 1 (3rd. ed.)*. https://www.fema.gov/sites/default/files/2020-03/publication-one_english_2019.pdf

United States Department of Homeland Security (US-DHS), Federal Emergency Management Agency (FEMA). (2021, September). Understanding the environment. In Developing and maintaining emergency operations plans: *Comprehensive preparedness guide (CPG) 101 (3rd ed.)*, pp.15-26. Washington, DC. https://www.fema.gov/sites/default/files/documents/fema_cpg-101-v3-developing-maintaining-eops.pdf

Walumbwa, F. O., Avolio, B. J., Gardner, W. L., Wernsing, T. S., & Peterson, S. J. (2008). Authentic leadership: Development and validation of a theory-based measure. *Journal of Management, 34*(1), 89-126. https://doi.org/10.1177/0149206307308913

Wallace, A. F. C. (1957). Human adaptation to disaster. *Human Organization, 16*(2), 23-27.

WHO/EHA. (2002). Disasters and emergencies: definitions. Retrieved from https://apps.who.int/disasters/repo/7656.pdf

World Health Organization. (2019, May 28) Burn-out an "occupational phenomenon": International Classification of Diseases. In *WHO.int*. Retrieved on June 10, 2022, from https://www.who.int/news/item/28-05-2019-burn-out-an-occupational-phenomenon-international-classification-of-diseases

Yukl, G. (1994). *Leadership in organizations* (3rd ed.). Prentice Hall.

About the Author

Carey H. Peerman is an assistant professor in the Department of Public Health and Healthcare Leadership at Radford University where she teaches health care administration. She has a PhD in organizational leadership from Concordia University and a master's degree in business administration from Radford University. Carey began her career in health care by earning a bachelor's degree in nursing from Radford University (1998). She also holds a certificate in health care administration-long term care from Mary Baldwin College and a certificate in executive leadership from the University of Notre Dame, Six Sigma Green Belt/Lean DFSS from Aventa, and a certificate in gerontology from The University of Texas at Austin.

A fellow in the American College of Health Care Executives, Carey is a licensed nursing home administrator and a registered nurse. She is also an active member of the Virginia Health Care Association and works as a health care consultant. She is the owner of Clear Edge Consulting, LLC.

Carey lives with her family in the mountains and valleys of Southwest Virginia where she is surrounded by extended family and many friends. She enjoys outdoor activities and traveling and is a lifelong learner.